This book is presented to:

....

From:

....

On:

....

May you embrace the power of prayer and always carry the promises of God in your heart.

For physical training is of some value, but godliness has value for all things, holding promise for both the present life and the life to come.

1 Timothy 4:8 NIV

The Power of Praying™
Copyright © 2004 by Stormie Omartian
Published by Harvest House Publishers
Eugene, Oregon 97402
www.harvesthousepublishers.com

Omartian, Stormie
  Power of praying / by Stormie Omartian.
     p. cm.
  ISBN 0-7369-1340-8
  1. Prayer—Christianity.   I. Title.
  BV210.3.053 2003
  242'.643--dc22

                                             2003015527

Text and prayers are taken from *The Power of a Praying® Woman*, *The Power of a Praying® Wife*, *The Power of a Praying® Parent*, and *Just Enough Light for the Step I'm On* by Stormie Omartian (Harvest House Publishers, 2002, 1997, 1995, and 1999).

Design and production by Koechel Peterson & Associates, Inc., Minneapolis, Minnesota

Unless otherwise indicated, all Scripture quotations are taken from the New King James Version. Copyright ©1982 by Thomas Nelson, Inc. Used by permission. All rights reserved.

Verses marked NIV are taken from the HOLY BIBLE, NEW INTERNATIONAL VERION®. NIV®. Copyright©1973, 1978, 1984 by the International Bible Society. Used by permission of Zondervan. All rights reserved.

Verses marked KJV are taken from the King James Version of the Bible.

Printed in the United States

04 05 06 07 08 09 10 / IP / 7 6 5 4 3

The POWER of PRAYING™

Help for a Woman's Journey Through Life

STORMIE OMARTIAN

HARVEST HOUSE PUBLISHERS

EUGENE, OREGON

$\mathcal{C}$ontents

His Divine Power

Today, more and more believing women are given an open door to become all they were created to be. They are moving out in different areas of expertise and ministry and making a difference. They are learning to rely on the power of God to prepare them and open the doors. They are realizing they are not just an afterthought in the order of God's creation. They were created for a special purpose.

So often we don't move into all God has for us because we don't understand what it is He has for us. If we don't know exactly what His promises are, we can't get a clear perspective of our situation. God's "divine power has given to us all things that pertain to life and godliness, through the knowledge of Him who called us by glory and virtue, by which have been given to us exceedingly great and precious promises, that through these you may be partakers of the divine nature" (2 Peter 1:3–4).

We need to know God's promises well enough to keep them perpetually in our minds and on our hearts. May these prayers and Scriptures help you do this.

When you live according to God's Word and by the power of His Holy Spirit, you can trust that you are in the right place at the right time and that the Lord is working His perfect will in your life. You can trust that God is moving you into the wholeness and blessing He has for you.

Stormie

Dear Lord,

Bless the woman who reads this book. Pour out Your Spirit upon her and help her to become all You created her to be. Give her a vision for her future and enable her to understand how great it is. Direct her steps so that she will always walk in the center of Your will. In Jesus' name I pray.

BEING A
WOMAN OF GOD

We can never draw close to God and get to know Him well, or develop the kind of intimate relationship we want, unless we spend time alone with Him. In those private times we are refreshed, strengthened, and rejuvenated. We can see our lives from God's perspective and discover what is really important as a woman of God. That's when we understand who it is we belong to and believe in.

When you find yourself praying to Him many times a day just because you love to be in His presence, then your relationship is growing deep.

Lord, may Your love manifested in me be a witness of Your greatness. Teach me to love others the way You do. Soften my heart where it has become hard. Make me fresh where I have become stale. Lead me and instruct me where I have become unteachable. Make me to be faithful, giving, and obedient the way Jesus was.

May Your light so shine in me that I become a light to all who know me. Make me to be so much like Christ that when people see me they will want to know You better.

✄ GOD'S PROMISE ✄

Therefore humble yourselves under the mighty hand of God, that He may exalt you in due time, casting all your care upon Him, for He cares for you.

1 Peter 5:6–7

GOD HAS SO MUCH TO SPEAK INTO YOUR LIFE. But
if you don't draw apart from the busyness of your day and spend
time alone with Him in quietness and solitude, you will not hear
it. Jesus Himself spent much time alone with God. If anyone
could get away with not doing it, surely it would have been
Him. How much more important must it be for us?

I know finding time alone to pray can be difficult. But if you
will make it a priority by setting a specific time to pray daily,
perhaps writing it in your calendar the way you would any other
important date, and determine to keep that standing appointment
with God, you'll see answers to your prayers like never before.

*Lord, I want to seek You today. I will never be happy until I
make You the source of my fulfillment and the answer to my
longings. You are the only one who should have power over
my soul. I look to You for everything I need—everyday. Help
me to put my expectations in You.*

∞ GOD'S PROMISE ∞
May He grant you according to your heart's desire,
and fulfill all your purpose.

Psalm 20:4

NURTURE YOUR SOUL

I WANT TO HELP YOU DRAW CLOSE TO YOUR HEAVENLY FATHER, to feel His arms around you, to maintain a right heart before Him, to live in the confidence of knowing that you are in the center of His will, to discover more fully who He made you to be, to find wholeness and completeness in Him, and to move into all He has for you.

In other words, I want to show you how to effectively cover your life in prayer so that you can have more of God in your life.

Dear Lord, open my eyes to see new treasures every time I read or hear Your word. Speak to me and comfort my heart. Make Your Word come alive in me and use it to nourish my soul and spirit like food does for my body. Align my heart with Yours and give me revelation and guidance so that I may know Your will for my life.

Shine the lamp of Your truth where I am right now and show me the next step to take.

❧ GOD'S PROMISE ❧

The entrance of Your words gives light;
It gives understanding to the simple.

Psalm 119:130

During my many speaking engagements over the past several years I took a survey to find out how women most wanted to be prayed for. Their response was unanimous in every city and state. The number one need of all women surveyed was that they would grow spiritually and have a deep, strong, vital, life-changing, faith-filled walk with God.

When we realize that it's Him that we want, we become free. We are free to identify the longings and emptiness inside of us as our signal that we need to draw near to God with open arms and ask Him to fill us with more of Himself. This deep and intimate relationship with God that we all desire doesn't just happen. It must be sought after, prayed for, nurtured, and treasured.

Lord, I pray that nothing will draw me away from fulfilling the plan You have for me. May I never stray from what You have called me to be and do. Give me a vision for my life and a strong sense of purpose. I put my identity in You and my destiny in Your hands. Show me if what I am doing now is what I am supposed to be doing. I want what You are building in my life to last for eternity.

❧ GOD'S PROMISE ❧
Draw near to God and He will draw near to you.

James 4:8

None of us enjoys going around in circles, always passing through the same territory and coming back to the same problems, same frustrations, same mistakes, and same limitations. We want to break out of self-defeating cycles and transcend ourselves, our limitations, and our circumstances. We want to be more than just a survivor.

We want to be an overcomer. We want to be a part of something greater than ourselves. We want to be connected to what God is doing on earth in a way that bears fruit for His kingdom. We want to abound in God's love and blessings. We want it all. All God has for us.

Lord, I don't want to be a spiritual underachiever. I want to be an overcomer. You paid a price for me so that I could be owned by You. Help me to live like it. You planned out a course for my life so that I could be defined by You. Help me to act like it. You made it possible for me to defeat my enemy. Help me not to forget it.

✎ GOD'S PROMISE ✎

Great peace have those who love Your law,
And nothing causes them to stumble.

Psalm 119:165

DO YOU EVER HAVE TIMES WHEN YOUR LIFE SEEMS OUT OF CONTROL? Do you ever feel pressured, as if your days are so busy that you fear you're missing out on a certain quality of life because of it? Do you worry that you are neglecting and not nourishing areas of your life because you are trying to fill numerous roles and meet many expectations?

Do you need to spend more time with God in prayer? Do you need a more complete knowledge of God's Word? Do you want to serve Him better and more completely but don't feel you have the time, energy, or opportunity? Do you ever just long to throw your arms wide open and embrace Jesus and feel His embrace of you? The good news is that this is the way God *wants* you to feel. He wants you to *want* Him.

Lord, help me to remember to live not in my own strength, but by the power of Your Spirit living in me. Forgive me for the times I have forgotten to do that. Enable me to grow in the things of Your kingdom so that I can become a whole, properly functioning, contributing, productive child of Yours who moves forward in Your purpose for my life.

❧ GOD'S PROMISE ❧

Trust in the LORD with all your heart, and lean not on your own understanding; in all your ways acknowledge Him, and He shall direct your paths.

Proverbs 3:5–6

LIVING THE ABUNDANT LIFE

IF YOU'RE LIKE ME, you don't want to live the kind of life where you are barely hanging on. You don't want to merely eke out an existence, find a way to cope with your misery, or just get by. You want to have the abundant life Jesus spoke of when He said, "I have come that they may have life, and that they may have it more abundantly" (John 10:10).

We don't want to be women who hear the truth but seldom act in faith to appropriate it for our lives. We don't want to be forever grappling with doubt, fear, insecurity, and uncertainty. We want to live life on purpose and with purpose. We want the solid food of God's truth so that we can grow into a life that is exciting and productive.

Lord, help me "to ask in faith, with no doubting." I know that a doubter is double-minded and unstable and will not receive anything from You (James 1:6–8). I confess any doubt I have as sin before You, and I ask You to forgive me. I don't want to hinder what You want to do in me and through me because of doubt. Increase my faith daily so that I can move mountains in Your name, and I can move into all You have for me.

∽ GOD'S PROMISE ∽
Without faith it is impossible to please Him,
for he who comes to God must believe that He is, and that
He is a rewarder of those who diligently seek Him.

Hebrews 11:6

Women all over the world want to live fruitful lives. They want to dwell in God's grace while still obeying His laws. They want to be unshakable in God's truth yet moved by the suffering and needs of others. They want to know God in all the ways He can be known, and they want to be transformed by the power of His Spirit. But they are quick to observe all they are doing wrong and slow to appreciate all they are doing right.

Look upon the idea of cleansing your heart not as a judgment that your heart is dirty, but as God's call for you to get completely right before Him so He can bring all the blessings He has for you into your life. Then you can know His abundance of peace, joy, love, and fulfillment.

Lord, I will prepare my heart by worshiping You and giving thanks in all things. Create in me a clean heart and a right spirit so that I will please You. Fill my heart with love, peace, and joy so that it will flow from my mouth. Convict me when I complain. I pray You would give me the words to say that will bring life and edification every time I speak to anyone.

✎ GOD'S PROMISE ✎

Beloved, if our heart does not condemn us, we have confidence toward God. And whatever we ask we receive from Him, because we keep His commandments and do those things that are pleasing in His sight.

1 John 3:21–22

Do you find it easier to pray for other people than it is to pray for yourself? I know *I* do. I can pray for my husband, my children, other family members, acquaintances, friends, and people I've never even met whom I hear about in the news far easier than I can pray for my own needs. For one thing, their needs are easy for me to identify. Mine are numerous, sometimes complicated, often difficult to determine.

We women know what we *think* we need most of the time. But we are often too emotionally involved in the people around us and the day-to-day existence of our lives to be able to figure out how we should be praying for ourselves. Sometimes we can be so overwhelmed by our circumstances that our prayer is simply a basic cry for help. But God's grace is all we need.

"Hear me when I call, O God of my righteousness! You have relieved me in my distress; have mercy on me, and hear my prayer" (Psalm 4:1). In times of suffering or trial, I pray for an added sense of Your presence. I want to grow stronger in these times and not weaker. I want to increase in faith and not be overcome with doubt. I want to stand strong in Your truth and grace.

☧ GOD'S PROMISE ☧
My grace is sufficient for you,
for My strength is made perfect in weakness.

2 Corinthians 12:9

GOD IS ALWAYS WANTING TO TAKE YOU TO A NEW
PLACE in your life, and you will keep Him from doing that if
you are hanging on to the way things have always been done. He
will never allow us to rest on past success. If we rely on the way
things have always been done, we aren't relying on *Him*. And
that's the whole point.

I guarantee that no matter how old you are, God has something
new He wants to do in your life. Ask Him to show you what
that is. Tell Him you intend to stay in the race and you don't
want to carry any baggage from the past around with you.

*Lord, help me to keep my eyes looking straight ahead and not
back on the former days and old ways of doing things. I know
You want to do something new in my life today. Help me to
concentrate on where I am to go now and not where I have
been. Thank You for releasing me from the past so that by Your
grace I can move out of it and into the future You have for me.*

❧ GOD'S PROMISE ❧
If anyone is in Christ, he is a new creation;
old things have passed away; behold, all things have become new.

2 Corinthians 5:17

TEN GOOD REASONS TO OBEY GOD

1. *We get our prayers heard.* "If I regard iniquity in my heart, the Lord will not hear. But certainly God has heard me; He has attended to the voice of my prayer" (Psalm 66:18–19).

2. *We enjoy a deeper sense of the Lord's presence.* "If anyone loves Me, he will keep My word; and My Father will love him, and We will come to him and make Our home with him" (John 14:23).

3. *We gain wisdom.* "He stores up sound wisdom for the upright; He is a shield to those who walk uprightly" (Proverbs 2:7).

4. *We have God's friendship.* "You are my friends if you do whatever I command you" (John 15:14).

5. *We can live safely.* "You shall observe My statutes and keep My judgments, and perform them; and you will dwell in the land in safety" (Leviticus 25:18).

6. *We are perfected.* "Whoever keeps His word, truly the love of God is perfected in Him. By this we know that we are in Him" (1 John 2:5).

7. *We are blessed.* "Behold, I set before you today a blessing and a curse: the blessing, if you obey the commandments of the LORD your God which I command you today" (Deuteronomy 11:26–27).

8. *We find happiness.* "Happy is he who keeps the law" (Proverbs 29:18).

9. *We have peace.* "Mark the blameless man, and observe the upright; for the future of that man is peace" (Psalm 37:37).

10. *We have a long life.* "My son, do not forget my law, but let your heart keep my commands; for length of days and long life and peace they will add to you" (Proverbs 3:1–2).

BLESSING YOUR FAMILY

*M*arriage is great when two people enter into it with a mutual commitment to keep it strong no matter what. But often a couple will have preconceived ideas about who the other is and how married life is supposed to be, and then reality hits. That's when their kingdom can become divided. You have to continually pray that unreal expectations be exposed and all incompatibilities be smoothed out so that you grow together in a spirit of unity, commitment, and a bond of intimacy.

Pray that your marriage is one in which you both agree and that God will be in the center of it.

> *Lord, unite my husband and me in a bond of friendship, commitment, generosity, and understanding. Eliminate our immaturity, hostility, or feelings of inadequacy. Help us to make time for one another alone, to nurture and renew our marriage and remind ourselves of the reasons we were married in the first place. I pray that my husband will be so committed to You, Lord, that his commitment to me will not waver, no matter what storms come.*
>
> *I pray that our love for each other will grow stronger every day.*

≈ GOD'S PROMISE ≈

Whatever God does, it shall be forever.
Nothing can be added to it, and nothing taken from it.

Ecclesiastes 3:14

I LEARNED THE BEST THING FOR OUR MARRIAGE
was for me to have women prayer partners with whom I prayed
every week. I believe this is vital for any marriage. If you can find
two or more strong, faith-filled women whom you thoroughly
trust, and with whom you can share the longings of your heart,
set up a weekly prayer time. It will change your life.

The purpose of such prayer is to ask God to make your heart
right, show you how to be a good wife, share the burdens of
your soul, and seek God's blessing on your husband.

*Lord, I pray You would protect our marriage from anything that
would harm or destroy it. Shield it from our own selfishness and
neglect, from the evil plans and desires of others, and from
unhealthy or dangerous situations. May there be no thoughts of
divorce or infidelity in our hearts, and none in our future.*

*I pray that there be no jealousy in either of us, or the low self-
esteem that precedes that. Let nothing come into our hearts and
habits that would threaten the marriage.*

❧ GOD'S PROMISE ❧

Two are better than one, because they have a good reward for their labor.
For if they fall, one will lift up his companion. But woe to him who is
alone when he falls, for he has no one to help him up.

Ecclesiastes 4:9–10

LIFTING UP YOUR HUSBAND

I THINK IF I COULD HELP A NEW WIFE in any area, it would be to discourage her from coming into her marriage with a big list of expectations and then being upset when her husband doesn't live up to them. Let go of the expectations. The changes you try to make happen in your husband, or that your husband tries to make in himself to please you, are doomed to failure and will bring disappointment for you both. Instead, ask God to make any necessary changes.

Accept your husband the way he is and pray for him to grow. Your greatest expectations must be from God, not from your husband.

Lord, I lay my expectations at Your cross. I release my husband from the burden of fulfilling me in areas where I should be looking to You. Help me to accept him the way he is and not try to change him. I realize, though, that because of Your working in him, he may change in ways I never thought he could.

I leave any changing that needs to be done in Your hands, fully accepting that neither of us is perfect and never will be. Only You, Lord, are perfect and I look to You to perfect us.

∽ GOD'S PROMISE ∽
My soul, wait silently for God alone,
for my expectation is from Him.

Psalm 62:5

The hard part about being a praying wife, other than the sacrifice of time, is maintaining a pure heart. It must be clean before God in order for you to see good results. That's why praying for a husband must begin with praying for his wife. If you have resentment, anger, unforgiveness, or an ungodly attitude, even if there's good reason for it, you'll have a difficult time seeing answers to your prayers.

But if you release those feelings to God in total honesty and then move into prayer, there is nothing that can change a marriage more dramatically.

God, I proclaim You Lord over my life. Help me to seek You first every day and set my priorities in perfect order. Reveal to me how to properly put my husband before children, work, family, friends, activities, and interests. Show me what I can do right now to demonstrate to him that he has this position in my heart. Mend the times I have caused him to doubt that.

Tell me how to prioritize everything so that whatever steals life away or has no lasting purpose will not occupy my time.

❧ GOD'S PROMISE ❧

Whatever things you ask when you pray, believe that you receive them, and you will have them. And whenever you stand praying, if you have anything against anyone, forgive him, that your Father in heaven may also forgive you your trespasses.

Mark 11:24–25

An important part of your job as a parent, or as a caretaker of a child, is to keep the details of your child's life covered in prayer. In doing this, I learned to identify every concern, fear, worry, or possible scenario that came into my mind as a prompting by the Holy Spirit to pray for that particular thing. As I covered my children in prayer and released them into God's hands, God released my mind from that concern.

God doesn't promise that nothing bad will ever happen to your child, but praying releases the power of God to work in his or her life, and you will enjoy more peace in the process.

Lord, I submit myself to You. I realize that raising up a child in the way You would have me to is beyond my human abilities. I know I need You to help me. I want to partner with You and partake of Your gifts of wisdom, discernment, revelation, and guidance. I also need Your strength and patience, along with a generous portion of Your love flowing through me.

Teach me to love the way You love.

∽ GOD'S PROMISE ∽
Pour out your heart like water
before the face of the Lord.
Lift your hands toward Him for the
life of your young children.

Lamentations 2:19

WHEN THINGS GO WRONG IN OUR CHILDREN'S LIVES, we blame ourselves for not being perfect parents. But I have found that it's not being a perfect parent that makes the difference in a child's life, because there are no perfect parents. It's being a *praying* parent that makes the difference. And that's something we *all* can be. In fact, we don't even have to be parents. We can be a friend, a teacher, a grandparent, a neighbor, or even a stranger with a heart of compassion.

If you are aware of a child who doesn't have a praying parent, you can step into the gap right now and answer that need. All it takes is a heart that says, "God, show me how to pray in a way that will make a difference in this child's life."

> *Lord, make me the parent You want me to be and teach me how to pray and truly intercede for the life of this child. Lord, You said in Your Word, "Whatever things you ask in prayer, believing, you will receive" (Matthew 21:22). In Jesus' name I ask that You will increase my faith to believe for all the things You've put on my heart to pray for concerning this child.*

∽ GOD'S PROMISE ∽

You did not choose Me, but I chose you
and appointed you that you should go and bear fruit,
and that your fruit should remain, that whatever you
ask the Father in My name He may give you.

John 15:16

CREATING A HOME WITH HEART

I DON'T CARE HOW LIBERATED YOU ARE, when you are married there will always be two areas that will ultimately be your responsibility: home and children. Even if you are the only one working and your husband stays home to keep the house and tend the kids, you will still be expected to see that the heart of your home is a peaceful sanctuary—a source of contentment, acceptance, rejuvenation, nurturing, rest, and love for your family.

On top of this, you will also be expected to be sexually appealing, a good cook, a great mother, and physically, emotionally, and spiritually fit. It's overwhelming to most women, but the good news is you can seek God's help.

Lord, help me to use the gifts You have given me to create a peaceful, restful, safe place for my family to live. Show me what to do and what not to do. I ask You to send Your Holy Spirit to dwell in my home so that all who enter in can sense Your peace and comfort. Help me to never do anything that would disturb the sanctuary-like qualities that are established there.

⤏ GOD'S PROMISE ⤎
Each one has his own gift from God,
one in this manner and another in that.

1 Corinthians 7:7

Part of making a house a home is allowing your husband to be the head so you can be the heart. Trying to be both is too much. God placed the husband as the head over the family, whether he deserves it or not and whether he rises up to take his position or not. It's God's order of things. This doesn't mean that one position is more important than the other. They work together.

This doesn't mean that the wife can't work and the husband can't care for the home; it's the attitudes of the heart and head that make the difference.

Lord, I pray that our commitment to You and to one another will grow stronger and more passionate every day. Enable him to be the head of the home as You made him to be, and show me how to support and respect him as he rises to that place of leadership. Help me to make our home a place he always wants to come back to.

Reveal to me what he wants and needs and show me potential problems before they arise. Come dwell in our home with us.

∞ GOD'S PROMISE ∞

Through wisdom a house is built, and by understanding it is established; by knowledge the rooms are filled with all precious and pleasant riches.

Proverbs 24:3–4

When you pray for your family, remember this model of a godly woman from the Bible. It says she takes care of her home and runs it well. She knows how to buy and sell and make wise investments. She keeps herself healthy and strong and dresses attractively. She works diligently and has skills which are marketable. She is giving and conscientiously prepares for the future. She contributes to her family's good reputation.

She is strong, solid, honorable, and not afraid of growing older. She speaks wisely and kindly. She carefully watches what goes on in her home. Her family praises her. She supports her family and still has a fruitful life of her own which speaks loudly for itself.

Lord, help me to be a good caretaker for my family. Take my selfishness, impatience, and irritability and turn them into kindness, long-suffering, and the willingness to bear all things. Give me a new heart and work in me Your love, peace, and joy. I am not able to rise above who I am. Only You can transform me.

❧ GOD'S PROMISE ❧
Let us not grow weary while doing good, for in due season
we shall reap if we do not lose heart.

Galatians 6:9

HOW MANY FAMILY RELATIONSHIPS ARE LEFT TO CHANCE BECAUSE NO ONE PRAYS ABOUT THEM? Far too many, I suspect. It's sad to see families split apart and individual members have nothing to do with one another when they are grown. It's heartbreaking to think of that happening with our own family. Yet it doesn't have to be that way.

"You shall raise up the foundations of many generations; and you shall be called the Repairer of the Breach" (Isaiah 58:12). God wants us to restore unity, to maintain the family bonds in the Lord, and to leave a spiritual inheritance of solidarity that can last for generations.

> *Lord, teach my family to resolve misunderstandings according to Your Word. And if any division has already begun, if any relationship is strained or severed, Lord, I pray that You will drive out the wedge of division and bring healing.*

> *Your Word instructs us to "be of one mind, having compassion for one another; love as brothers, be tenderhearted, be courteous" (1 Peter 3:8). In Jesus' name I pray that You would instill a love and compassion in all family members that is strong and unending, like a cord that cannot be broken.*

≋ GOD'S PROMISE ≋
Behold, how good and how pleasant
it is for brethren to dwell together in unity!

Psalm 133:1

FIVE GOOD WAYS TO PRAISE THE LORD

God wants us to give our whole self to worshiping Him, and He wants us to do it *His* way.

1. *God wants us to sing our praises to Him.* "Praise the Lord! For it is good to sing praises to our God; for it is pleasant, and praise is beautiful" (Psalm 147:1). "Serve the Lord with gladness; come before His presence with singing" (Psalm 100:2).

2. *God wants us to lift our hands to Him.* "Lift up your hands in the sanctuary, and bless the Lord" (Psalm 134:2).

3. *God wants us to speak our praise to Him.* "Therefore by Him let us continually offer the sacrifice of praise to God, that is, the fruit of our lips, giving thanks to His name" (Hebrews 13:15).

4. *God wants us to praise Him with dancing and instruments.* "Let them praise His name with the dance; let them sing praises to Him with the timbrel and harp" (Psalm 149:3).

5. *God wants us to praise Him together with other believers.* "I will declare Your name to My brethren; in the midst of the assembly I will sing praise to You" (Hebrews 2:12).

UNDERSTANDING HIS PROMISES

God has great plans for you. He has important things He wants you to do. And He is preparing you for your destiny right now. But you have to trust that He knows the way and won't hurt you in the process.

God's rules are for our benefit, not to make us miserable. When we live by them, life works. When we don't, life falls apart. When we obey, we have clarity. When we don't, we have confusion. If you have become frustrated because you don't see answers to your prayers, ask God if it is because of disobedience. Say, "Lord, is there any area of my life where I am not living Your way?" Don't keep telling God what *you* want without asking Him what *He* wants.

> Lord, show me what You want me to do today to be a blessing to others around me. Specifically, show me how I can serve my family, my friends, my church, and the people whom You put in my life. I don't want to get so wrapped up in my own life that I don't see the opportunity for ministering Your life to others. I want to fulfill Your plans for my life.

∾ GOD'S PROMISE ∾

For the LORD God is a sun and shield;
the LORD will give grace and glory;
no good thing will He withhold from those
who walk uprightly.

Psalm 84:11

YOU NEVER KNOW WHEN YOU WILL STEP INTO THE MOMENT for which God has been preparing you. And it is not just one moment; it's many successive ones. It doesn't matter whether you are a single career woman or a married lady with nine children under the age of ten; it doesn't matter whether you are nineteen or ninety, God is preparing you daily for something great.

He wants you to be willing to let Him purify you, fortify you, and grow you up in Him. But you have to play by the rules. "If anyone competes in athletics, he is not crowned unless he competes according to the rules" (2 Timothy 2:5). You can't move into the mainstream of those moments successfully if you are not doing what He wants you to do now.

> *God, show me Your will for my life and help me to move into it. Help me to learn Your ways and walk in your paths. I don't ever want to get off of the path You have for me. I want to fulfill all Your plans for my life.*

❧ GOD'S PROMISE ❧

Come, and let us go up to the mountain of the LORD,
To the house of the God of Jacob;
He will teach us His ways,
And we shall walk in His paths.

Micah 4:2

SEE THAT HE IS ALWAYS THERE

WHEN GOD USED MOSES to lead the Israelites out of Egypt, they had to learn to depend on the Lord for every step of their journey to the Promised Land. When they did not do that, they got into trouble. It's the same for us today. God moves us out on a path to someplace we've never been before, and we believe we are failing if we have to depend on Him to get there. We need to trust that He will always be there.

We try to make it on our own because we think that dependency is a sign of weakness, instead of understanding that it signals our willingness to allow God to be strong in us. If you are at a place in your life where you feel like you can't take one step without the Lord's help, be glad. He has you where He wants you.

> *Lord, I am home wherever You are. If you call me into the wilderness, I will embrace it because You are there with me. Help me to not walk in fear or doubt, but in faith. Shine Your light on the path You have for me to travel. Help me to trust You are always with me.*
>
> *Forgive me when I grumble or have less than a grateful heart about where I am right now. I know my attitude will have a direct bearing on whether I wander around in circles, or whether I get through to the Promised Land You have for me.*

∾ GOD'S PROMISE ∾
The steps of a good man are
ordered by the LORD,
And He delights in his way.

Psalm 37:23

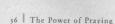

Refusing to walk according to God's leading will get you nowhere. Oh, you will arrive someplace all right, but if it is not where God wants to bless you, it will still be nowhere.

It doesn't matter what your situation is at this moment. Wherever you are, God has a path for you that is filled with good things. Draw close to Him and you'll find it. Say, "Show me the way in which I should walk and the thing I should do" (Jeremiah 42:3). He will do that and, if you carefully follow as He guides you, He will not let you get off the path. With each step He will reveal more of Himself. Reach up right now and take God's hand. He promises to always be there and to never let you fall.

I know that when I try to run the race without You, I get off course. So I commit this day to walk Your way. Thank You that even if I become weak and stumble, You will help me to rise again and continue on. Thank You that You will never leave me or forsake me.

Although I can't see exactly where I am going, I'm certain that You can and will enable me to get to where I need to be. Thank You, Lord, that You are teaching me how to walk in total dependence upon You, for I know therein lies my greatest blessing.

∽ GOD'S PROMISE ∽
Your ears shall hear a word behind you, saying,
"This is the way, walk in it."

Isaiah 30:21

Everything is dark until light is brought into it. If we don't have the true light, we live in darkness. But if we have the light in us that cannot be extinguished, which is the light of the Lord, then we can never be in total darkness.

There are different kinds of darkness, however, and we need to be able to discern one from the other. There is spiritual darkness that happens when we refuse to let God enter into our lives. There is the darkness of negative emotions like ignorance, pride, jealousy, anger, or hatred. Yet as damaging as our mistakes can be, God gives us a way out of the darkness we get ourselves into.

Lord, thank You that because I walk with You I don't have to fear the dark. Even in the blackest night, You are there. In the darkest times, You have treasures for me. No matter what I am going through, Your presence and grace are my comfort and my light. Thank You that You have brought us out of darkness and into Your glorious light.

❧ GOD'S PROMISE ❧

Then they cried out to the LORD in their trouble, and He saved them out of their distresses. He brought them out of darkness and the shadow of death, and broke their chains in pieces.

Psalm 107:13–14

THINK ABOUT WHAT IT'S LIKE WHEN THE POWER GOES OUT IN YOUR HOME AT NIGHT. You can barely function in the dark. You walk carefully, one step at a time, reaching out for familiar things to steady and guide you until you can find a flashlight, candle, or generator switch. If someone is holding a source of light, you reach out and take their hand so you can move together. You don't take a step until you're certain that both of you are going in the same direction.

That's exactly how God uses darkness in our lives. We're in the dark until we see *His* light in it. He wants us to reach out for Him so we can walk together in the same direction.

Lord, I believe in You and know that You have lifted me out of the darkness of hopelessness, futility, and fear. I refuse to be afraid. Help me to never walk in the darkness of doubt, disobedience, or blaming You for my circumstances.

I extend my hand to You, Lord. Take hold of it and lead me. Thank You that as I take each step, the light You give me will be all I need.

✎ GOD'S PROMISE ✎

Who walks in darkness and has no light?
Let him trust in the name of the LORD
And rely upon his God.

Isaiah 50:10

DEVELOP YOUR PERSONAL RELATIONSHIP

WHEN I DON'T TAKE ENOUGH TIME FOR GOD AND ME ALONE, I become so depleted I cannot go on. I feel like an eggshell, as if I could be crushed with very little outside pressure. I know I need more of God in my life, and nothing on earth is more important than that. There isn't anything else that can satisfy the hunger I feel inside except more of His presence.

It is important to guard and protect your personal relationship with God in prayer. Pray about every aspect of your life in such a manner that it will keep you spiritually anchored and reminded of what God's promises are to you. It will keep you focused on who God is and who He made you to be.

Lord, You are my light and my salvation. You are the strength of my life. Of whom, then, shall I be afraid? I will be strong and of good courage, for I know that You are with me wherever I go.

If I have gotten my mind off of You and on my circumstances, help me to reverse that process so that my mind is off my circumstances and on You. Because I have received a kingdom which cannot be shaken, may I have grace by which to serve You acceptably with reverence and godly fear all the days of my life.

∞ GOD'S PROMISE ∞
If anyone thirsts, let him come to Me and drink.
He who believes in Me, as the Scripture has said,
out of his heart will flow rivers of living water.

John 7:37–38

Jesus is Lord whether we declare it or not. But He is not only Lord over the universe, He is Lord over our individual lives as well. If we don't personally declare Jesus to be Lord over our lives, it shows we are not controlled by the Spirit. Whether or not you acknowledge that Jesus is Lord over your life will determine the success and quality of your life.

God doesn't want just part of you. He wants all of you. Pray that you will give God what He wants.

> *God, help me to say yes to You immediately when You give me direction for my life. My desire is to please You and hold nothing back. I surrender my relationships, my finances, my work, my recreation, my decisions, my time, my body, my mind, my soul, my desires, and my dreams. I put them all in Your hands so they can be used for Your glory. I want You to be Lord over every area of my life.*

> *Lord, I pray that You will rule in every area of my life and lead me into all that You have for me.*

❧ GOD'S PROMISE ❧

Those who wait on the LORD shall renew their strength; they shall mount up with wings like eagles, they shall run and not be weary, they shall walk and not faint.

Isaiah 40:31

Do you have trouble remembering names? I know I do. I can remember faces and names separately, but I don't always put the right ones together. And that can get me into trouble. With God it's a different situation. He has only one face, but many, many names. If we don't know all of His names, we may not understand all the aspects of His character. We may forget one just when we need to remember it.

For example, we may think of God as our Comforter, but forget that He is our Deliverer. We might think of Him as our Protector, but fail to remember Him as our Healer. Some people never think of God beyond being their Savior. But God wants to be even more than that to us. He wants us to know all the aspects of His character because the way we recognize God will affect the way we live our lives.

Lord, I praise Your name this day for You are good and Your mercy endures forever. Forgive me when I neglect to praise and worship You as You deserve and desire. Teach me to worship You with my whole heart the way You want me to. Make me a true worshiper, Lord.

I worship You in the splendor of Your holiness and give You the glory due Your name.

∼ GOD'S PROMISE ∼

Until now you have asked nothing in My name.
Ask, and you will receive, that your joy may be full.

John 16:24

THE WORD "JESUS" WHEN SPOKEN IN LOVE BY ONE WHO REVERENCES HIM, HAS GREAT POWER IN IT. Power to save, deliver, heal, provide, protect, and so much more. There is also great power in each one of God's names, and when spoken with faith, love, understanding, and reverence, it brings a blessing and increases your faith.

God's name is always a safe place to run to any time you need help. If you are sick, run to your Healer. If you can't pay your bills, run to your Provider. If you are afraid, run to your Hiding Place. If you are going through a dark time, run to your Everlasting Light. By speaking His name with reverence and thanksgiving, you invite Him to be that to you.

Lord, I thank You that there is power in Your name. Thank You that Jesus has been given "the name which is above every name, that at the name of Jesus every knee should bow" (Philippians 2:9–10). Thank You that I can reach out and touch You and in turn be touched by the power of Your name.

✎ GOD'S PROMISE ✎

The name of the LORD is a strong tower;
the righteous run to it and are safe.

Proverbs 18:10

THIRTY GOOD NAMES TO CALL YOUR GOD

1. Healer (Psalm 103:3)
2. Redeemer (Isaiah 59:20)
3. Deliverer (Psalm 70:5)
4. My Strength (Psalm 43:2)
5. Shelter (Joel 3:16)
6. Friend (John 15:15)
7. Advocate (1 John 2:1)
8. Restorer (Psalm 23:3)
9. Everlasting Father (Isaiah 9:6)
10. Love (1 John 4:16)
11. Mediator (1 Timothy 2:5–6)
12. Stronghold (Nahum 1:7)
13. Bread of Life (John 6:35)
14. Hiding Place (Psalm 32:7)
15. Everlasting Light (Isaiah 60:20)
16. Strong Tower (Proverbs 18:10)
17. Resting Place (Jeremiah 50:6)
18. Spirit of Truth (John 16:13)
19. Refuge from the Storm (Isaiah 25:4)
20. Eternal Life (1 John 5:20)
21. The Lord Who Provides (Genesis 22:14)
22. Lord of Peace (2 Thessalonians 3:16)
23. Living Water (John 4:10)
24. My Shield (Psalm 144:2)
25. Husband (Isaiah 54:5)
26. Helper (Hebrews 13:6)
27. Wonderful Counselor (Isaiah 9:6)
28. The Lord Who Heals (Exodus 15:26)
29. Hope (Psalm 71:5)
30. God of Comfort (Romans 15:5)

BUILDING FOUNDATIONS OF FAITH

When I started learning to pray about every aspect of my life, I asked God to help me be disciplined enough to be daily in His Word, to pray faithfully, and to take the steps of obedience I needed to take. I asked Him to deliver me from depression and anything else that kept me from all He had for me. I was surprised at how quickly God answered those prayers. I have become disciplined, organized, and obedient beyond what I believe are my natural capabilities.

As a result of obeying God in new ways, my spirit is renewed with each passing year. And with each new step of obedience I take, I experience new blessings and new freedoms I have not known before and never thought possible.

Lord, Your Word says that "if we say we have no sin, we deceive ourselves, and the truth is not in us" (1 John 1:8). I don't want to deceive myself by not asking You where I am missing the mark You have set for my life. Reveal to me when I am not doing things I should be doing. Show me if I'm doing things I should not.

❧ GOD'S PROMISE ❧

He who has My commandments and keeps them,
it is he who loves Me. And he who loves Me will be loved
by My Father, and I will love him and manifest Myself to him.

John 14:21

WE CAN NEVER BE PRIDEFUL about how perfectly we are obeying God because He is continually stretching us and asking us to move into new levels of growth. Nor can we go to the other extreme, saying "This is just the kind of person I am— undisciplined and unteachable." We have no excuse for not doing what we need to do when God says He will enable us to do it if we will just call upon Him for help.

All we have to say is, "Lord, help me to be disciplined enough to obey You the way You want me to so I can become the person You created me to be." Without the perfecting, balancing, refining work of His Holy Spirit, the freedom you have in Christ will turn into a license to do anything you want.

Oh, Lord, help me to hear Your specific instructions to me. Speak to me clearly through Your Word so I will know what's right and what's wrong. I don't want to grieve the Holy Spirit in anything I do (Ephesians 4:30). Help me to be ever learning about Your ways so I can live in the fullness of Your presence and move into all You have for me.

∾ GOD'S PROMISE ∾
Blessed are those who hear the word of God and keep it!

Luke 11:28

CONFESSION

SIN IS HARD TO AVOID 100 PERCENT OF THE TIME. That's why confession is crucial. When we don't confess our sins, faults, or errors, they separate us from God. And we don't get our prayers answered. "Your iniquities have separated you from your God; and your sins have hidden His face from you, so that He will not hear" (Isaiah 59:2).

When we don't confess our sins, we end up trying to hide ourselves from God. Just like Adam and Eve in the garden, we feel we can't face Him. But the problem with attempting to hide from God is that it's impossible. The Bible says that everything we do will be made known. The sooner we deal with the sins we can see, the sooner God can reveal to us the ones we can't.

Lord, I confess any unforgiveness in my heart for things that have happened in the past, and I release all persons who are associated with it. Heal all misunderstandings or hurts that have happened. Give me Your revelation and show me all I need to see in order to walk out of the shadow of my past sins and into the light You have for me today.

❧ GOD'S PROMISE ❧
If we confess our sins, He is faithful
and just to forgive us our sins
and to cleanse us from all unrighteousness.

1 John 1:9

*I*t's best to confess every sin as soon as we are aware of it and get our hearts cleansed and right immediately. Confession gets sin out in the open before God. When you confess your sin, you're not informing God of something He doesn't know. He already knows. He wants to know that *you* know.

Confession is more than just apologizing. Anyone can do that. We all know people who are good apologizers because they get so much practice. In fact, they sometimes say, "I'm sorry" without ever actually admitting to any fault. But true confession means admitting in full detail what you have done and then fully repenting of it.

> *Lord, everything I have done and all that was done to me I lay at Your feet. I give You my bad memories and ask that You would heal me to complete wholeness so that they no longer hurt, torment, or control me. I give You my past failures. Deliver me from them. Even though I may be unable to completely resist the pull of certain things on my own, I know You are able to set me free. Make me a testimony to the power of Your healing and deliverance.*

✄ GOD'S PROMISE ✄
He who covers his sins will not prosper, but whoever confesses and forsakes them will have mercy.

Proverbs 28:13

REPENTANCE

*I*t's one thing to recognize when you have done something that has violated God's laws; it's another to be saddened by it to such a degree that you are determined to never do it again. Repentance means to change your mind. To turn and walk the other way. Repentance means being so deeply sorry for what you have done that you will do whatever it takes to keep it from happening again.

Confession means we recognize we have done wrong and admit our sin. Repentance means we are sorry about our sin to the point of grief, and we have turned and walked away from it. Ask God every day to show you where your heart is not clean and right before Him. Don't let anything separate you from all God has for you.

> *Lord, enable me to deny myself in order to take up my cross daily and follow You. I want to be Your disciple just as You have said in Your Word (Luke 14:27). Help me to do what it takes. I want to lose my life in You so I can save it. Teach me what that means. Speak to me so that I may understand.*

❧ GOD'S PROMISE ❧

Repent therefore and be converted, that your sins may be blotted out, so that times of refreshing may come from the presence of the Lord.

Acts 3:19

**REPENTING OF SOMETHING DOESN'T NECESSARILY
MEAN WE WILL NEVER COMMIT THAT SIN AGAIN.**
It means we don't *intend* to ever commit it again. So if you find
that you have to confess the same sin again after you have only
recently confessed and repented of it, then do it. Confess and
repent as many times as necessary and see yourself win the battle
over this problem.

Don't entertain thoughts such as, *Surely God won't forgive me
again for the same thing I just confessed to Him last week.* He
forgives every time you confess sins before Him and fully repent
of it. You can turn things around in your life when you turn to
the Lord and repent.

> *Lord, help me to separate myself from anything that is not holy.
> I don't want to waste my life on things that have no value. Give
> me discernment to recognize that which is worthless and remove
> myself from it.*

> *Help me not to give myself to impure things but rather to those
> things that fulfill Your plans for my life. Enable me to do what
> it takes to get everything rooted out of my life that is not Your
> best for me, so I can live the way You want me to live. Help me
> to examine my ways so that I can return to Your ways wherever
> I have strayed.*

✎ GOD'S PROMISE ✎
Blessed is he whose transgression is forgiven,
whose sin is covered.

Psalm 32:1

SURRENDER

I KNOW A YOUNG MAN WHO HAS A HEART FOR GOD and is tremendously gifted to lead worship and teach the word. But he can't bring himself to fully surrender his life to the Lord. He continues doing his own thing and then is frustrated when nothing works out. If he would just say, "Whatever You want, Lord, I will do it," and truly live that out, God would use him powerfully and every part of his life would be blessed.

Why do some people never seem to grow in the Lord? Or never experience the release to step out in the area of their gifting? The answer, I believe, lies in the word "surrender." If they would drop everything and say, "I give up, Lord. I surrender. Take everything. I will do whatever You say," their lives would be better in every way.

Lord, I bow before You this day and declare that You are Lord over every area of my life. I surrender myself and my life to You and invite You to rule in every part of my mind, soul, body, and spirit. I love You with all my heart, with all my soul, and with all my mind.

I commit to trusting You with my whole being. I declare You to be Lord over every area of my life today and every day.

❧ GOD'S PROMISE ❧

If we live, we live to the Lord; and if we die, we die to the Lord. Therefore, whether we live or die, we are the Lord's.

Romans 14:8

Why is it so hard for us to simply say, "Whatever You want, Lord. I'll do anything You ask"? It's because we want what we want and we're afraid of what God might ask of us. We think He might do something to hurt us. Also, it's not just a matter of saying, "Jesus is Lord." We must then do what He says. Jesus said, "Why do you call Me 'Lord, Lord,' and do not do the things which I say?" (Luke 6:46).

If you feel you aren't experiencing any breakthrough in your life, check to see if you have truly surrendered yourself to the Lord. Have you given Jesus that place of lordship? Have you let go of everything? If not, lift your hands and take that first step.

Lord, whatever You want me to do, I'll do it. I say yes to anything You ask of me, even though it means dying to myself and my desires. I will give up the things of the flesh that I want in order to have more of You in my life.

I will go to church when I feel like staying home. I will pray when I would rather go to bed. I will read Your Word when I would rather watch TV. I will give when I would rather spend my money on myself. I will enter into praise and worship as my first reaction. I will strive to please You and move into all You have for me.

⟶ GOD'S PROMISE ⟵

If anyone desires to come after Me, let him deny himself,
and take up his cross daily, and follow Me.
For whoever desires to save his life will lose it,
but whoever loses his life for My sake will save it.

Luke 9:23–24

Being holy is not being perfect. It's letting Him who is holy be in you. We can't be holy on our own, but we can make choices that allow holiness and purity to be manifested in our lives. We can separate ourselves from that which dilutes God's holiness in us. And we can do this because "those who are Christ's have crucified the flesh with its passions and desires" (Galatians 5:24). We are able to live pure lives consecrated to the Lord.

There comes a time in all of our lives when we are desperate to know that God is close and that He hears our prayers and will answer. We won't have time to get right with God; we will have to *be* right with God. Now is the time to start living righteous, pure, and holy lives if we want to see our prayers answered in the future.

Lord, You have said in Your Word that You did not call me to uncleanness, but to holiness. You chose me to be holy and blameless before You. I know that I have been washed clean and made holy by the blood of Jesus. Help me to live in the Spirit and not the flesh.

You have clothed me in Your righteousness and enabled me to put on the new man "in true righteousness and holiness" (Ephesians 4:24). Continue to purify me by the power of Your Spirit. Help me to cling to what is good and keep myself pure.

❧ GOD'S PROMISE ❧
He who sows to the Spirit will of the Spirit reap everlasting life.

Galatians 6:8

IT IS ONLY BY THE GRACE OF GOD THAT WE CAN LIVE IN HOLINESS, even after we have chosen to do so. That's because God enables us to do what He asks us to do. But we still need to ask Him to do it. God wants to know that His holiness is important enough to us to seek after it. This doesn't mean we don't have to be concerned about sin anymore and can do whatever we want because He took care of it. It means we must continue to dwell with Him and ask God to help us live in all He bought for us on the cross.

People are drawn to holiness because it is attractive, even though they may resist it in their lives. Ask God to enhance your beauty with the beauty of His holiness.

Lord, I want to be holy as You are holy. Make me a partaker of Your holiness and may my spirit, soul, and body be kept blameless. I know that You have called me to purity and holiness. Thank You that You will keep me pure and holy so I will be fully prepared for all You have for me.

∾ GOD'S PROMISE ∾

Blessed are the pure in heart, for they shall see God.

Matthew 5:8

SEVEN GOOD WAYS TO LIVE IN HOLINESS

1. *Holiness means separating yourself from the world.* This doesn't mean you head for the hills, isolate yourself, and never speak to a nonbeliever. It means your heart detaches from the world's value system. You, instead, value the things God values above all else.

2. *Holiness means purifying yourself.* Purifying yourself does not mean putting on a white robe to cover up all that is not holy about you. It means asking God, who is holy, to purify your heart.

3. *Holiness means living in the Spirit and not in the flesh.* Our fleshly thoughts will disqualify us as much as our actions. Pray that God will help you live in the Spirit and not the flesh.

4. *Holiness means staying clear of sexual immorality.* The greatest lie our society has blindly accepted is that sexual sin is okay. Ask God to keep you sexually pure in your mind, soul, and body.

5. *Holiness means being sanctified by Jesus.* Once we have received Jesus, we can't continue to live our old sinful lifestyle. Now that we have Him living in us and the Holy Spirit guiding us and transforming us, we have no excuse.

6. *Holiness means walking close to God.* When we do not pursue a close walk with God and a lifestyle of purity and peace, we are unable to see the Lord with any kind of clarity. "Pursue peace with all people, and holiness, without which no one will see the Lord" (Hebrews 12:14).

7. *Holiness means letting God keep you.* Holiness is not something you slip in and out of like a nightgown. Holiness is God's will for our lives, and something God has planned for us from the beginning. God has made a way for us to live in holiness. And He is able to *keep* us holy. When our heart wants to live in purity and do the right thing, God will keep us from falling into sin.

FACING TRIALS

LEARNING DEPENDENCE

MORE AND MORE, GOD IS TEACHING ME TO
TRUST HIM FOR EVERY STEP I TAKE. He constantly
calls me to stretch beyond what's comfortable. To walk
through new territory when I would rather stay with the
familiar. To face difficult physical, mental, and emotional
challenges. To do things I know I can't achieve by myself
without His power.

I trust Him for each day of life, grateful for every breath,
determined to look for the blessing in the moment, no
matter what the circumstances. I follow His lead—even
when I can't see where I'm going, even when it scares me to
do so—because deep within my spirit I know that these
simple steps of faith are preparing me for eternity.

*Lord, I depend on You for everything. I give up my inde-
pendence. Help me to get beyond myself and become an
open vessel through which Your light can shine. Give me
Your wisdom and revelation and show me all I need to see
to keep me on the road You have for me. Enable me to step
out of my past and keep an eye on my eternal future with
You. Help me to follow You as You light my path today.*

❧ GOD'S PROMISE ❧
They need no lamp nor light of the sun,
for the Lord God gives them light.

Revelation 22:5

Let's get something straight. That is, you and I are not perfect. No one is perfect. None of us is incapable of sin. None of us is without problems. None of us have walked so long with the Lord that we know it all and therefore have nothing to learn. None of us is so complete that we don't need anything from God. None of us has it all together.

There! It's out in the open. We know it about ourselves and we know it about each other. Therefore, we can be completely honest with ourselves about ourselves. When we embrace this truth, we can then embrace the freedom of being dependent on God.

Lord, help me not be anxious about my future but to rest in the knowledge that my future is secure in You. I want to keep one foot in eternity by never letting go of Your hand. I want to store up so many treasures in heaven that heaven will feel familiar the moment I arrive. And when I do take that final step into my eternal future with You, I trust that You will be there for me for that step too. Help me depend on You all the days of my life.

⤳ GOD'S PROMISE ⤳
He who trusts in his own heart is a fool,
but whoever walks wisely will be delivered.

Proverbs 28:26

How many times in your life have you found yourself waiting? Waiting for things to change, more money, a better relationship, the right door to open, the right person to come along, for somebody to notice you. We don't like waiting. But God says waiting can be good, because that's how we learn patience.

God says we need patience because it makes us complete. That's because patience is one of the attributes of God. When we are patient, we are like Him. When we are tested, walking in the wilderness, surrendering our dreams, or standing in the line of fire, part of what we are learning is to be patient.

Lord, I wait upon You this day. I put my hope in Your Word and ask that You would fill me afresh with Your Holy Spirit and wash away all anxiety or doubt. Shine Your spotlight into any dark corner of my soul that needs to be exposed. I don't want my impatience or lack of trust to stand in the way of all You desire to do in me. Help me be patient, Lord. Help me to be like You.

∾ GOD'S PROMISE ∾
Those who wait on the LORD
Shall renew their strength;
They shall mount up with wings like eagles,
They shall run and not be weary,
They shall walk and not faint.

Isaiah 40:31

IN ADDITION TO PRAYING, there are other things you can do to keep your season of waiting on the Lord from turning into a dark time. Stay in God's Word and keep learning about Him. Ask the Lord to show you the talents and abilities He has given you and how you should develop them. Ask Him to reveal anything you need to start or stop doing. Perhaps He is waiting on *you*.

If you continue to walk with God and take the steps you know are right, you will get where you need to go. It may seem like forever, but don't be discouraged. God has been known to do a quick work for which He has been preparing a long time. Let Him sustain you in the interim. Tell yourself that you will "Rest in the LORD, and wait patiently for Him..." (Psalm 37:7).

I realize, Lord, that even when my life seems to be standing still, as long as I cling to You I am moving forward on the path You have for me. As I wait on You, help me to grow in my understanding of Your ways, and not succumb to impatience or discouragement because my timetable does not coincide with Yours.

Strengthen my faith to depend on Your perfect timing for my life. Help me to rest in You and be content with the step I'm on and the light You have given me.

GOD'S PROMISE
Wait on the LORD; be of good courage,
And He shall strengthen your heart.

Psalm 27:14

PERSEVERING IN FAITH

REMEMBER, IF YOU HAVEN'T BEEN PRAYING MUCH, you can't expect things to change overnight. It takes a while to get the enormous ocean liner of your life turned around and headed in a different direction. In fact, you may hardly see any changes at first. It's the same way with prayer. Prayer can turn your life around, but it doesn't always happen the moment you utter your first words.

Don't give up just before your breakthrough into the realm of answered prayer. Remember, this trip is not a mini-vacation tour around the harbor; it's a lifelong voyage to meet your destiny. Giving up is not an option.

Lord, I lift to You the things that frighten me most and ask that You would protect me and the people I love from them. I know that my enemy is the one who "has made me dwell in darkness...Therefore my spirit is overwhelmed within me...Cause me to know the way in which I should walk, for I lift up my soul to You" (Psalm 143:3–4,8).

Give me wisdom, strength, and clarity of mind to hear what You are saying to me in the midst of any dark or overwhelming situation. May my life be a testimony of the power of Your glory manifested as I walk in the light You have given me.

∾ GOD'S PROMISE ∾
The Lord is my light and my salvation;
whom shall I fear? The Lord is the strength of my life;
of whom shall I be afraid?

Psalm 27:1

Keep in mind that the greater your commitment is to the Lord, the more the devil will try to harass you. That's why if you are moving into a deeper level of commitment to God, or coming into a new time of deliverance and freedom, or entering into new ministry or work God is opening up for you, you can depend on your enemy trying to stop it.

He will try to get you to give up. Even though he is not close to being as powerful as God, he attempts to make you think otherwise. He will try to convince you he is winning the battle, but the truth is that he has already lost. Don't let the enemy of your soul talk you into accepting anything less than what God has for you.

Lord, I thank You for suffering and dying on the cross for me, and for rising again to defeat death and hell. I believe my enemy is defeated because of what You have done. Thank You that You have given me all authority over him. I have faith that by the power of Your Holy Spirit I can successfully resist the devil and he must flee from me.

Show me when I am not moving in faith. Teach me to use that authority You have given me to see the enemy defeated in every area of my life.

❧ GOD'S PROMISE ❧
If you have faith as a mustard seed,
you will say to this mountain,
"Move from here to there," and it will move;
and nothing will be impossible for you.

Matthew 17:20

Being filled with the Holy Spirit is not something that happens against our will. It is something we have to be open to, something we must desire, something for which we have to ask. We have a choice about whether we will be filled with the Holy Spirit or not. God wants us to desire Him. He wants us to desire His indwelling spirit.

Recognize the Holy Spirit of God as the power of God, and ask God to fill you with His Holy Spirit so He can empower you to move into all He has for you.

> *Lord, I want to live my life the way You want me to every day. Help me not to be stuck in my past, or so geared toward the future that I miss the richness of the present. Help me to experience the wealth in each moment. I don't desire to take a single step apart from Your presence. Fill me afresh with Your Holy Spirit this day. Guide me in the way You want me to go. If You're not moving me, I'm staying here until I have a clear leading from You.*

❧ GOD'S PROMISE ❧

If you then, being evil, know how to give good gifts to your children, how much more will your heavenly Father give the Holy Spirit to those who ask Him!

Luke 11:13

WHEN YOU FIND IT DIFFICULT TO DO WHAT YOU KNOW YOU NEED TO, ask the Holy Spirit to help you. Of course, you still have to take the first step, no matter how daunting, intimidating, dreadful, uncomfortable, or distasteful. But when you do, the Holy Spirit will assist you the rest of the way.

Years ago, God instructed my husband and me to move from California to Tennessee. This was not something I wanted to do. But because it was a clear directive from God, we packed up and obeyed. The reasons why we moved have become increasingly evident over the years, and I am so grateful we heard God's directive and followed it. But we probably wouldn't have heard if we hadn't actually said the words, "Lord, show us what we are supposed to be doing."

> *Lord, I thank You for Your Word. It is food to my soul, and I cannot live without it. Enable me to truly comprehend its deepest meaning. Give me greater understanding than I have ever had before, and reveal to me the hidden treasures buried there. Speak to my heart all that You want me to know. Give me ears to hear Your voice.*

❧ GOD'S PROMISE ❧
He who heeds the word wisely will find good,
and whoever trusts in the LORD, happy is he.

Proverbs 16:20

FOUR GOOD REASONS FOR DIFFICULT TIMES

1. *Sometimes difficult things happen to us so that the glory and power of God can be revealed in and through us.* When Jesus passed by a man who was born blind, His disciples asked Him if the man's blindness was because he had sinned or because his parents had sinned. Jesus replied, "Neither this man nor his parents sinned, but that the works of God should be revealed in him" (John 9:3). We may not be able to understand why certain things are happening at the time, and we may never know why we have to go through them until we go to be with the Lord, but when we turn to God in the midst of difficult situations, His glory will be seen in them and on us.

2. *God uses difficult times to purify us.* The Bible says, "Since Christ suffered for us in the flesh, arm yourselves also with the same mind, for he who has suffered in the flesh has ceased from sin" (1 Peter 4:1). This means our suffering during difficult times will burn sin and selfishness out of our lives. God allows suffering to happen so that we will learn to live for Him and not for ourselves. So that we will pursue His will and not our own. It's not pleasant at the time, but God's desire is "that we may be partakers of His holiness" (Hebrews 12:10). He wants us to let go of the things we lust after and cling to what is most important in life—Him.

3. *Sometimes our misery is caused by God disciplining us.* "No chastening seems to be joyful for the present, but painful; nevertheless, afterward it yields the peaceable fruit of righteousness to those who have been trained by it" (Hebrews 12:11). The fruit that this godly disciplining and pruning produces in us is worth the trouble we have to go through to get it, and we have to be careful not to resist it or hate it. "Do not despise the chastening of the Lord, nor be discouraged when you are rebuked by Him; for whom the Lord loves He chastens, and scourges every son whom He receives" (Hebrews 12:5–6).

4. *Sometimes we are caught in the midst of the enemy's work.* It's the enemy's delight to make you miserable and try to destroy your life. Often the reason for the anguish, sorrow, sadness, grief, or pain you feel is entirely his doing and no fault of your own or anyone else's. Your comfort is in knowing that as you praise God in the midst of it, He will defeat the enemy and bring good out of it that you can't even fathom. He wants you to walk with Him in faith as He leads you through it, and He will teach you to trust Him in the midst of it.

Moving Toward the Future

God has a great future planned for you. I know this because He said so. He says you have not seen, nor heard, nor even imagined anything as great as what He has prepared for you (1 Corinthians 2:9).

Remember, God "is able to do exceedingly abundantly above all that we ask or think, according to the power that works in us" (Ephesians 3:20). Stay focused on God, and He will keep you in perfect peace as He moves you into the future He has for you.

Lord, I put my future in Your hands and ask that You would give me total peace about it. I don't want to be trying to secure my future with my own plans. I want to be in the center of Your plans, knowing that You have given me everything I need for what is ahead. I pray You would give me strength to endure without giving up.

Thank You, Holy Spirit, that You are always with me and will guide me on the path so that I won't lose my way. I cast all my cares upon You, knowing that You care for me and will not let me fall. I reach out for Your hand today so I can walk with You into the future You have for me.

❧ GOD'S PROMISE ❧
There is surely a future hope for you,
and your hope will not be cut off.

Proverbs 23:18

IF YOU BECOME ANXIOUS ABOUT YOUR FUTURE, or you need encouragement about what is ahead, listen to God as He speaks to your heart. You will hear Him say that what He has for you is so great that if you truly understood it, you would feel "that the sufferings of this present time are not worthy to be compared with the glory which shall be revealed" in you (Romans 8:18). That means whatever you envision for your life right now is already too small.

Although we live in a world where everything in our lives can change in an instant, and we can't be certain what tomorrow will bring, God is unchanging. You may not know the specific details about what is ahead, yet you can trust that God knows. And He will get you safely where you need to go. In fact, the way to get to the future God has for you is to walk with Him today.

> *Lord, help me to run the race in a way that I shall finish strong and receive the prize You have for me. Help me to be always watchful in my prayers, because I don't know when the end of my life will be.*

> *I know that You have saved me and called me with a holy calling, not according to my works, but according to Your own purpose and grace. Move me into powerful ministry that will impact the lives of others for Your kingdom and Your glory. I humble myself under Your mighty hand, O God, knowing that You will lift me up in due time.*

❧ GOD'S PROMISE ❧
I know the thoughts I think toward you, says the LORD,
thoughts of peace and not of evil, to give you a future and a hope.

Jeremiah 29:11

A HIGH PURPOSE

EACH ONE OF US HAS A PURPOSE IN THE LORD.
But many of us don't realize that. And when we don't have
an accurate understanding of our identity, we either strive to
be like someone else or something we're not. We compare
ourselves to others and feel as though we always fall short.

God doesn't want that for you. He wants you to have a clear
vision for your life. He wants to reveal to you what your
gifts and talents are and show you how to best develop
them and use them for His glory.

*Lord, I thank You that You have called me with a holy
calling, not according to my works, but according to Your
purpose and grace which was given to me in Christ Jesus
(2 Timothy 1:9). I know that Your plan for me existed
before I knew You, and You will bring it to pass. I know
there is an appointed plan for me, and I have a destiny
that will now be fulfilled.*

*So I pray that You would show me clearly what the gifts
and talents are that You have placed in me. Lead me in the
way I should go as I grow in them. Enable me to use them
according to Your will and for Your glory.*

❧ GOD'S PROMISE ❧

In Him also we have obtained an inheritance, being predestined
according to the purpose of Him who works all things according
to the counsel of His will, that we who first trusted in Christ
should be to the praise of His glory.

Ephesians 1:11–12

We all need to have a sense of why we are here. We all need to know we were created for a purpose. We will never find fulfillment and happiness until we are doing the thing for which we were created. But God won't move us into the big things He has called us to unless we have proven faithful in the small things He has given us. So if you are doing what you deem to be small things right now, rejoice! God's getting you ready for the big things ahead.

May you never forget that God has an important purpose for your life and that it is good.

Lord, help me to understand the call You have on my life. Take away any discouragement I may feel and replace it with joyful anticipation of what You are going to do through me. Use me as Your instrument to make a positive difference in the lives of those whom You put in my path. Help me to rest in the confidence of knowing that Your timing is perfect.

I put my identity in You and my destiny in Your hands. Show me if what I am doing now is what I am supposed to be doing. I want what You are building in my life to last for eternity.

∞ GOD'S PROMISE ∞

Be even more diligent to make your call and election sure,
for if you do these things you will never stumble.

2 Peter 1:10

Wisdom means having clear understanding and insight. It means knowing how to apply the truth in every situation. It's discerning what is right and wrong. It's having good judgment. It's being able to sense when you are getting too close to the edge. It's knowing how to make the right choice or decision. And only God can give you that kind of wisdom.

We have no idea how many times simple wisdom has saved our lives or kept us out of harm's way or how many times it will do so in the future. That's why we can't live without it and need to ask God for it.

> Lord, give me Your wisdom and understanding in all things. I know wisdom is better than gold and understanding better than silver (Proverbs 16:16), so make me rich in wisdom and wealthy in understanding. Increase my wisdom and knowledge so I can see Your truth in every situation.
>
> I don't want to trust my own heart. I want to trust Your Word and Your instruction so that I will walk wisely and never do ignorant or stupid things. Lord, I know that in You "are hidden all the treasures of wisdom and knowledge" (Colossians 2:3). Help me to discover those treasures.

✎ GOD'S PROMISE ✎
Call to Me, and I will answer you, and show you great
and mighty things, which you do not know.

Jeremiah 33:3

GOD SEES ALL BECAUSE HE IS ABOVE ALL. If we were to connect with Him on a regular basis and say, "Lord, guide me so I won't fall," He could lead us away from the edge. But so often we don't make that connection with God. We don't call. We don't seek His guidance. We don't ask Him for wisdom. We don't consider His perspective. And too often we fall off the path because of it.

Have you ever observed someone with no wisdom clearly doing the wrong thing or making a foolish decision? A friend? A family member? A peer? The consequences are crystal clear to you but *they* don't see it at all. It's always easier to see a lack of wisdom in others than it is to see it in ourselves. That's why we must pray daily for wisdom. Take time to get God's perspective of your life and circumstances.

Lord, help me to always seek godly counsel and not look to the world and ungodly people for answers. Thank You, Lord, that You will give me the counsel and instruction I need.

I delight in Your law and in Your Word. Help me to meditate on it day and night, to ponder it, to speak it, to memorize it, to get it into my soul and my heart. Lord, I know that whoever "trusts in his own heart is a fool, but whoever walks wisely will be delivered" (Proverbs 28:26). Help me to walk uprightly, righteously, and obediently to Your commands. Keep me far from evil so that I can claim the health and strength Your Word promises.

⟋ GOD'S PROMISE ⟍
You have made known to me the path of life;
you will fill me with joy in your presence,
with eternal pleasures at your right hand.

Psalm 16:11 NIV

A TIME TO SEEK GOD

BEFORE I CAME TO KNOW THE LORD, I was involved in all kinds of occult practices and Eastern and New Age religions. I searched for God in each one of them hoping to find some meaning or purpose for my life.

However, those gods I was chasing were distant, cold, remote, and did not have the power to save or transform a human life. But the God of the Bible did! He is the one, true, living God. And when we find Him and receive Him, His Spirit dwells in us.

I learned that He is a God who can be found. A God who can be known. A God who wants to be close to us. That's why He is called Immanuel, which means "God with us." We must take the time to seek and draw close to the one who desires to be with you.

Lord, I draw close to You today, grateful that You will draw close to me as You have promised in Your Word. I long to dwell in Your presence, and my desire is for a deeper and more intimate relationship with You. I want to know You in every way You can be known. Teach me what I need to learn in order to know You better.

I am open to whatever You want to do in me. I don't want to limit You by neglecting to acknowledge You in every way possible. I declare this day that You are my Healer, my Deliverer, my Redeemer, and my Comforter. I seek to know You better each day.

❧ GOD'S PROMISE ❧
Draw near to God and He will draw near to you.

James 4:8 NIV

If I could sit down and talk with you in person about your life, I would tell you that if you have received the Lord, the answer to what you need is within you. That's because the Holy Spirit of God is within you, and He will lead you in all things. He will transform you and your circumstances beyond your wildest dreams if you will give up trying to do it on your own and let Him do it His way.

We all long for the closeness, the connection, the affirmation that we are good and desirable. But God is the only one who can give all that to you all of the time. Your deepest needs will only be met in an intimate relationship with Him. No one can ever know you as well or love you as much. That insatiable longing for more than you feel, the emptiness you want those closest to you to fill, is put there by God so that He can fill it.

Lord, help me to set aside time each day to meet with You alone. To seek You. Enable me to resist all that would keep me from it. Teach me to pray the way You want me to. Help me to learn more about You. I thirst for more of You because I am in a dry place without you.

I know You are everywhere, but I also know that there are deeper manifestations of Your presence that I long to experience. Draw me close so that I may dwell in Your presence like never before.

⤞ GOD'S PROMISE ⤝
Jesus stood and said in a loud voice,
"If anyone is thirsty, let him come to me
and drink. Whoever believes in me, as the Scripture has said,
streams of living water will flow from within him."

John 7:37–39 NIV

On my tenth birthday, I received a necklace that consisted of a small glass ball hanging from a delicate gold chain. Inside the ball was the tiniest mustard seed. I thought at the time, *Why in the world did they bother putting a seed in there that was so small it could hardly be seen?* It wasn't until later that I learned the significance of that necklace. Jesus tells us that if we have faith the size of a mustard seed, we have enough faith to move mountains!

God takes the tiniest bit of faith we have and makes it grow into something big when we act on it. The Bible says that "God has dealt to each one a measure of faith" (Romans 12:3) We already have some faith to start with! When we step out in that faith, God *increases* our faith.

> *Lord, increase my faith. Teach me how to "walk by faith, not by sight" (2 Corinthians 5:7). Give me strength to stand strong on Your promises and believe Your every word. I know that "faith comes by hearing, and hearing by the word of God" (Romans 10:17).*

> *Make my faith increase every time I hear or read Your Word. Help me to believe that Your promises will be fulfilled in me. I pray that the genuineness of my faith will be glorifying to you, Lord.*

∽ GOD'S PROMISE ∽

He replied, "Because you have so little faith. I tell you the truth,
if you have faith as small as a mustard seed,
you can say to this mountain,
'Move from here to there' and it will move.
Nothing will be impossible for you."

Matthew 17:20 NIV

EVERY DAY IT BECOMES MORE AND MORE CRUCIAL THAT WE HAVE FAITH. There will be times in each of our lives when we will need the kind of faith that makes the difference between success or failure, winning or losing, life or death. That's why asking for more faith must be an ongoing prayer. No matter how much faith you have, God can increase it.

What promise of God would you like to claim in faith? What would you like to see accomplished in your life, or in the life of someone you know, that would take a prayer of great faith? Ask God to take that little seed and grow it into a giant tree of faith so you can see these things come to pass.

Lord, I know "faith" is the substance of things hoped for, the evidence of things not seen." I know I have been "saved through faith," and it is a gift from You. Increase my faith so that I can pray in power. Give me faith to believe for healing every time I pray for the sick. I don't want to see a need and then not have faith strong enough to pray and believe for the situation to change.

I confess any doubt I have as sin before You, and I ask You to forgive me. I don't want to hinder what You want to do in me and through me because of doubt. Increase my faith daily so that I can move mountains in Your name.

❧ GOD'S PROMISE ❧
All things are possible to him who believes.

Mark 9:23

TEN GOOD REASONS TO ASK FOR WISDOM

1. *To enjoy longevity, wealth, and honor.* "Length of days is in her right hand, in her left hand riches and honor" (Proverbs 3:16).

2. *To have a good life.* "Her ways are ways of pleasantness, and all her paths are peace" (Proverbs 3:17 niv).

3. *To enjoy vitality and happiness.* "She is a tree of life to those who take hold of her, and happy are all who retain her" (Proverbs 3:18).

4. *To secure protection.* "Then you will walk safely in your way, and your foot will not stumble" (Proverbs 3:23).

5. *To experience refreshing rest.* "When you lie down, you will not be afraid; yes, you will lie down and your sleep will be sweet" (Proverbs 3:24).

6. *To gain confidence.* "For the Lord will be your confidence, and will keep your foot from being caught" (Proverbs 3:26).

7. *To know security.* "Do not forsake her, and she will preserve you; love her, and she will keep you...when you walk, your steps will not be hindered, and when you run, you will not stumble" (Proverbs 4:6,12).

8. *To be promoted.* "Exalt her, and she will promote you; she will bring you honor, when you embrace her" (Proverbs 4:8).

9. *To be protected.* "When wisdom enters your heart, and knowledge is pleasant to your soul, discretion will preserve you; understanding will keep you, to deliver you from the way of evil, from the man who speaks perverse things" (Proverbs 2:10–12).

10. *To gain understanding.* "A wise man will hear and increase learning, and a man of understanding will attain wise counsel" (Proverbs 1:5).

FOLLOWING GOD'S LEAD

Have you ever found yourself angry, upset, or devastated when things didn't turn out as you'd hoped or planned? Next time that happens, look deeply into the situation and ask God to give you a new perspective.

Because we walk in the light of the Lord, blessings abound for us in each moment. Sometimes, though, we have to deliberately look for them. My daughter, Mandy, and I have developed a plan for seeing the truth whenever something goes wrong. We look at the situation and ask, "What's right with this picture?" We pray for God to show us how what we think of as a negative situation is actually a positive one.

This is not just positive thinking or trying to make good things happen with your thoughts. This is seeing things from God's perspective and letting Him show you the truth.

Lord, I lift to You the situations of my life that concern me. I lay my worries before You and ask for Your mighty intervention to show me what's right when I can only see what's wrong. I am determined to see the good, so help me not to be blinded by my own fears, doubts, wants, and preconceived ideas. I ask You to reveal to me Your truth in every situation.

✎ GOD'S PROMISE ✎

And we know that all things work together
for good to those who love God,
to those who are the called according to His purpose.

Romans 8:28

LOOK AT YOUR LIFE RIGHT NOW. Is there anything that worries or upsets you? If so, say, "Lord, show me what's right with this picture. What is the truth in this moment? Help me to see it from Your perspective." You'll be amazed at what God reveals.

If your attitude is one of gratefully searching for God's truth and goodness in any situation, it will change your life. You'll never see things the same way again. No matter what happens, you'll be able to say, "This was our Lord's doing." It is a matter of trust. It's basically believing that God is good and He desires the best for you. Give God the benefit of your trust and you'll see that you are standing in more light than you ever dreamed possible.

Lord, give me Your perspective today and for my future. Bless me with the ability to understand the bigger picture and to distinguish the valuable from the unimportant. When something seems to go wrong, help me not to jump to negative conclusions. Enable me to recognize the answers to my own prayers.

Let me trust You, Lord, in all things and for all things. When I look at my life and my circumstances, may I see the good work that You are doing.

⤳ GOD'S PROMISE ⤳
Oh, taste and see that the LORD is good;
blessed is the man who trusts in Him!

Psalm 34:8

GOD'S WILL, YOUR CALLING

THERE IS A CALL FROM GOD ON YOUR LIFE AND MINE. The question is, will we listen to find out what it is? I've seen many people who were too busy, too tired, too preoccupied, or too in pursuit of riches and fame to hear God calling them. I've known others who heard the call of God but ran away from it.

If you feel called to something better than what you are doing now, let me assure you that it is probably because you are. If you have never sought God about His plans and purposes for your life, do that. Know that He will not leave you where you are forever. Just seek His will and listen for the call.

Lord, I know You have great purpose for me and a plan for my life. Open my ears to hear Your voice leading me into all You have for me. Align my heart with Yours and prepare me to understand where You would have me to go and what You would have me to do.

Help me to hear Your call. I will listen for Your voice now. I don't want to be unfruitful and unfulfilled because I never clearly heard Your call. I want You to fill me with Your greatness so that I may do great things for others as You have called me to do. I commit to walking this road step by step with You so that I may fully become all that You have made me to be.

⊷ GOD'S PROMISE ⊷

...whom He predestined, these He also called; whom He called, these He also justified; and whom He justified, these He also glorified.

Romans 8:30

We all want to be in the center of God's will. That's why we shouldn't pursue a career, a move to another place, or any major life change without the knowledge that it is the will of God. We must regularly ask God to show us what His will is and lead us in it. We must ask Him to speak to our heart so He can tell us.

The best place to start seeking God's will for your life is "in everything give thanks; for this is the will of God in Christ Jesus for you" (1 Thessalonians 5:18). Thank Him for keeping you in the center of His will. Then ask Him to guide your every step. It feels so good to be confident you are on the right path and doing what God wants.

Lord, help me to walk in a worthy manner, fully pleasing to You, being fruitful in every good work and increasing in the knowledge of Your ways. Guide my every step. Lead me "in Your righteousness" and "make Your way straight before my face" (Psalm 5:8). As I draw close and walk in intimate relationship with You each day, I pray You will get me where I need to go.

Lord, align my heart with Yours. Help me to hear Your voice. Speak to me from Your Word so that I will have understanding. If there is something I should be doing, reveal it to me so that I can correct my course. I want to move into all You have for me and become all You made me to be by walking in Your perfect will for my life now.

∼ GOD'S PROMISE ∼

Whether you turn to the right or to the left, your ears will hear
a voice behind you, saying, "This is the way; walk in it."

Isaiah 30:21–22 NIV

We can't live successfully without right priorities in our lives. Yet some of us try to do that every day. Correct priorities are not something we can figure out on our own. We have to be led by the Holy Spirit and have a clear knowledge of God's Word in order to understand what we should be.

Our two most important priorities come directly from the Word of God. Jesus told us about them saying, "'You shall love the LORD your God with all your heart, with all your soul, and with all your mind.' This is the first and great commandment. And the second is like it: 'You shall love your neighbor as yourself'" (Matthew 22:37–39). If you maintain these two top priorities—love God and love others—they will guide you in setting all the other priorities in your life.

Lord, I pray You would help me set my life in right order. I want to always put You first above all else in my life. Teach me how to love You with all my heart, mind, and soul. I don't want to have any other gods but You in my life.

Show me if I have lifted up my soul to an idol. My desire is to serve You and only You. Help me to live accordingly.

❧ GOD'S PROMISE ❧

Seek first the kingdom of God and His righteousness,
and all these things shall be added to you.

Matthew 6:33

YOUR RELATIONSHIP WITH THE LORD MUST ALWAYS HAVE TOP PRIORITY over everything else. The Lord said, "You shall have no other gods before Me" (Exodus 20:3), and He means it. God wants your undivided attention. When you seek Him first every day and ask Him to help you put your life in order, He will do that.

God is a God of order. We can tell that by looking at the universe. None of it is random or accidental. He doesn't want our lives to be either. And when we pray to Him about it, He will help us do just that. He will show us how to align ourselves under proper authority so that we can come under the covering of His protection. This is crucial to our moving into all God has for us.

Lord, I know that if my life is not in proper order, I will not receive the blessings You have for me. But I also know that if I seek You first, all that I need will be added to me.

I seek You first this day and ask that You would enable me to put my life in perfect order. May I never come out from under the covering of spiritual protection You have placed in my life. Each day I will rise to make You first and others second, Lord.

⧉ GOD'S PROMISE ⧉

He who finds his life will lose it,
and he who loses his life for My sake will find it.

Matthew 10:39

KEEP YOUR MIND ON GOD

DO CERTAIN NEGATIVE THOUGHTS PLAY OVER AND OVER IN YOUR MIND? Do "what if" thoughts ever plague you? Or perhaps you dwell on "if only" regrets that cause you to question each decision you make. Do you ever think "No one cares about me." "Nothing ever turns out right for me." If you have had these thoughts, please know that this is not God giving you revelation for your life. These are words spoken to our souls by an enemy.

We can overcome each of these lies with prayer, faith, and the truth of God's Word. When we fill our minds with God's Word and resources written by people in whom God's Spirit resides, and we listen to music that praises and glorifies Him, we leave no room for anything else.

Lord, help me to never exchange Your truth for a lie. Where I have accepted a lie as truth, reveal that to me. I don't want to think futile and foolish thoughts or give place to thoughts that are not glorifying to You.

May Your Word be so etched in my mind that I will be able to identify a lie of the enemy the minute I hear it. Spirit of Truth, keep me undeceived. I refuse to listen to lies. I want to fill my mind and my life with Your truths, Your love, and Your Word.

❧ GOD'S PROMISE ❧
You will keep him in perfect peace, whose mind
is stayed on You, because he trusts in You.

Isaiah 26:3

You have a choice about what you will accept into your mind and what you won't. You can choose to take every thought captive and "let this mind be in you which was also in Christ Jesus" (Philippians 2:5).

You don't have to live with confusion or mental oppression. You don't have to "walk as the rest of the Gentiles walk, in the futility of their mind, having their understanding darkened, being alienated from the life of God, because of the ignorance that is in them, because of the blindness of their heart" (Ephesians 4:17–18). Instead you can have clarity and knowledge that comes from the Lord.

Thank You, Lord, that I "have the mind of Christ" (1 Corinthians 2:16). I want Your thoughts to be my thoughts. Show me where I have filled my mind with anything that is ungodly. Help me to resist doing that and instead fill my mind with thoughts, words, music, and images that are glorifying to You. Help me to think upon what is true, noble, just, pure, lovely, of good report, virtuous, and praiseworthy.

I lay claim to the "sound mind" that You have given me, Lord.

❧ GOD'S PROMISE ❧

Do not be conformed to this world, but be transformed by the renewing of your mind, that you may prove what is that good and acceptable and perfect will of God.

Romans 12:2

Life is a walk. Each day we take steps. Our tomorrow is determined by the steps we take today. When we learn to walk with our heavenly Father, He wants us to reach up and take His hand, but He doesn't want us to ever let go. In fact, His desire is that we become more and more dependent upon Him for every step. That's because He wants to take us to places we've never been. To heights we can't even imagine.

If you are headed in the wrong direction, He will turn you around. If you have come to a standstill, He will get you moving. As you take one step at a time, holding God's hand and letting Him lead, He will get you where you need to go.

> *Lord, lead me in the path You have for me. From this day on I want to walk with You. I take this step of faith and I trust You to meet me here. Align my heart with Yours. I trust that no matter where I am right now, even if I have gotten off course, You will guide me.*
>
> *I love that your grace abounds to me in that way. I love that I can rest in the knowledge that You have a direction for my life.*

✎ GOD'S PROMISE ✎

O LORD, I know the way of man is not in himself;
it is not in man who walks to direct his own steps.

Jeremiah 10:23

LEARNING TO WALK WITH GOD IS A PROCESS. And just when we think we have it all figured out, God leads us to a new place where our old tricks won't work. In fact, it may seem like we're learning how to walk all over again. And in a way we are. We enter unfamiliar territory and are soon reminded that, on our own, we stumble.

Yet when we take His hand, we fly. God wants us to soar far above the limitations of our lives and ourselves. How exciting that He wants to accomplish great things through you that can only come out of a life of faith. When you hear God guiding you to move in a certain direction, let me give you two words of advice: *Do it!*

Lord, thank You that even if I become weak and stumble, You will help me to rise again and continue on. And though I can't see exactly where I am going, I'm certain that You can and will enable me to get to where I need to be. Thank You that You are teaching me how to walk in total dependence upon You, for I know therein lies my greatest blessing.

Remind me that when I feel I am failing…and having to rely on You alone…that is when I am truly living the way I should. Turn my heart toward dependence on You.

∽ GOD'S PROMISE ∽
You will show me the path of life;
In Your presence is fullness of joy;
At Your right hand are pleasures forevermore.

Psalm 16:11

FOUR GOOD THINGS THAT ARE TRUE ABOUT GOD'S WILL

1. *Following God's will does not mean we will never have trouble.* Trouble is a part of life. Having fulfillment and peace in the midst of trouble is what living in God's will is all about. There is great confidence in knowing that you are walking in the will of God and doing what He wants you to do. When you are sure of that, you can better deal with what life brings you. So don't think that trouble in your life means you are out of God's will. God uses the trouble you have to perfect you. There is a big difference between being out of God's will and being pruned or tested by God. Both are uncomfortable, but in one, you will have peace, no matter how uncomfortable it gets. In the other, you won't.

2. *Following God's will is not easy.* The life of Jesus confirms that following God's will is not always fun, enjoyable, pleasant, or easy. Jesus was doing God's will when He went to the cross. He said, "For I have come down from heaven, not to do My own will, but the will of Him who sent Me" (John 6:38). If anyone could have said, "I don't want to follow God's will today," I think it would have been Him. But He did it perfectly. And now He will enable us to do it too.

3. *Following God's will can make you very uncomfortable.* In fact, if you don't ever feel stretched or uncomfortable in your walk with the Lord, then I would question whether you are actually in the will of God. It has been my personal experience that stretched and uncomfortable is a way of life when walking in the will of God.

4. *Following God's will doesn't happen automatically.* That's because God gave us a choice as to whether we subject our will to Him or not. We make that decision every day. Will we seek His will? Will we ask Him for wisdom? Will we do what He says? "Do not be unwise, but understand what the will of the Lord is" (Ephesians 5:17). God's will is the way we choose to live each day of our lives.

ENJOYING GIFTS ALONG THE WAY

We all need deliverance at one time or another. That's because no matter how spiritual we are, we're still made of flesh. And no matter how perfectly we live, we still have an enemy who is trying to erect strongholds of evil in our lives. God wants us free from everything that binds, holds, or separates us from Him.

So often we live our lives as if we don't realize Jesus paid an enormous price so we could be free. Jesus "gave Himself for our sins, that He might deliver us from this present evil age, according to the will of our God and Father" (Galatians 1:4). He wants to continue to set us free in the future.

Lord, thank You for promising to "deliver me from every evil work and preserve me" for Your heavenly kingdom (2 Timothy 4:18). Without You I am held captive by my desires, I am blind to the truth, and I am oppressed. But with You comes freedom from all that. "My times are in Your hand; deliver me from the hand of my enemies, and from those who persecute me" (Psalm 31:15).

Help me to stand fast in the liberty by which Christ has made me free.

✦ GOD'S PROMISE ✦
The righteous cry out, and the LORD hears,
and delivers them out of all their troubles.

Psalm 34:17

**YOU FIND FREEDOM WHEN YOU PRAY FOR DELIV-
ERANCE.** Pray for it yourself, have someone else who is a
strong believer pray with you for it, read the truth of God's
Word with great understanding and clarity, and spend time in
the Lord's presence. The most effective and powerful way to
spend time in the Lord's presence is in praise and worship.

God wants you free not only because He loves you and has
compassion upon you, but because He wants you to be able to
"serve Him without fear, in holiness and righteousness before
Him," all the days of your life (Luke 1:74–75). Deliverance won't
change you into someone else. It will release you to be who you
really are—an intelligent, secure, loving, talented, kindhearted,
witty, attractive child of God.

*Lord, I call upon You and ask that You would deliver me from
anything that binds me or separates me from You. Give me
wisdom to walk in the right way and strength to rise above the
things that would pull me down.*

*I know that You who have begun a good work in me will
complete it. Give me patience to not give up and the strength to
stand strong in Your Word. Make darkness light before me and
the crooked places straight. You are my deliverer, Lord. I praise
You and thank You for setting me free.*

❧ GOD'S PROMISE ❧

Deliver me in Your righteousness, and cause me to escape;
incline Your ear to me, and save me.

Psalm 71:2

HIS LIGHT

KING DAVID WAS A MAN WHO WENT THROUGH SOME VERY DARK TIMES. Some of them were his fault, and some of them weren't. In either case, David always knew that the light on his path came from God. He was still God's anointed no matter how dark it got. Even when he made bad choices, he had a heart for the Lord. And God never allowed him to be destroyed.

It's the same with those of us who love God. His light is always available to us. No matter how badly we think we've blown it in our lives, we are never truly in darkness when we look to Him. God's light is constant because *He* is constant.

Lord, I trust that You are the light of my life. You are unchanging. And because You never change, Your light is constant in my life no matter what is going on around me. I give this day to You and trust that the light You give me is just the amount I need for the step I'm on.

❧ GOD'S PROMISE ❧

This is the message which we have heard from Him and declare to you, that God is light and in Him is no darkness at all. If we say that we have fellowship with Him, and walk in darkness, we lie and do not practice the truth. But if we walk in the light as He is in the light, we have fellowship with one another, and the blood of Jesus Christ His Son cleanses us from all sin.

1 John 1:5–7

Whenever we go through dark and difficult times, we anticipate the coming moment when all the pressure is off, the worry has subsided, the healing has manifested, the sadness has lifted, and the pain is gone. We continuously look for God to take away the discomfort we are experiencing. But God wants us to know that even as we wait for those changes to happen, He is already there. His light can be found in the darkest night.

So don't worry about seeing or understanding what the future holds. God wants you to trust Him as He leads you, even though you can't see clearly ahead. And don't be overly concerned about fully comprehending the past. Only He knows the whole truth about it anyway. You have *Him* now. He is your light. And that is all that matters.

Lord, grow me up in Your ways and lead me in Your will. Help me to become so strong in You that I will not waver or doubt. Help me to trust the light of Your Word in even the darkest nights of my soul.

I pray that I will always have a teachable heart that recognizes Your hand in my life and soaks up Your instruction. Help me trust Your timing. Establish in me an unwavering faith so that when I walk with You I will not doubt Your ways and Your love.

☙ GOD'S PROMISE ❧
I will make darkness light before them,
and crooked places straight…and not forsake them.

Isaiah 42:16

I used to think that living with anxiety, depression, fear, and hopelessness was a way of life. *This is just the way I am,* I thought. But when I came to know the Lord and started living God's way, I began to see that *all* things are possible to anyone who believes and obeys God. It's even possible to live without negative emotions. God will take them off of us. But we have to pray.

We all have difficult times when we feel all alone and abandoned. But the truth is we aren't. God is with us to help us when we call upon Him. In the midst of these times, we don't have to be controlled by our negative emotions. We can resist them by praying and knowing the hope of what God's Word says about them.

> *Lord, help me to live in Your joy and peace. Give me strength and understanding to resist anxiety, anger, unrest, envy, depression, bitterness, loneliness, fear, and guilt. Rescue me when "my spirit is overwhelmed within me; my heart within me is distressed" (Psalm 143:4). I refuse to let my life be brought down by negative emotions. I know You have a better quality of life for me than that. When I am tempted to give in to them, show me Your truth. Your hope.*

∾ GOD'S PROMISE ∾

Be anxious for nothing, but in everything by prayer and supplication,
with thanksgiving, let your requests be made known to God;
and the peace of God, which surpasses all understanding,
will guard your hearts and minds through Christ Jesus.

Philippians 4:6–7

THE MOST IMPORTANT WORDS WE CAN SPEAK ARE ONES THAT EXPLAIN OUR FAITH to anyone who asks or who will listen. We must be able to give a reason for the hope we have within us. We have to pray that God will help us become bold enough to clearly explain our faith in God. We have to ask God to help us tell others why we call Jesus our Messiah, why we can't live without the Holy Spirit, and why we choose to live God's way.

If the love of God and the testimony of His goodness and hope are not in our heart, then they will not come out of our mouth. And we will miss the opportunity to share our greatest gift.

Lord, help me to be a person who speaks words that build up and not tear down. Help me to speak life and hope into the situations and people around me. Fill my heart afresh each day with Your Holy Spirit so that Your love and goodness overflow from my heart and my mouth.

Give me words that speak of the hope that is within me so I can explain my faith in a compelling way. May the words I speak bring others into a fuller knowledge of You.

∽ GOD'S PROMISE ∽

But even if you should suffer for righteousness' sake, you are blessed.
And do not be afraid of their threats nor be troubled.
But sanctify the LORD God in your hearts,
and always be ready to give a defense to everyone
who asks you to give a reason for the hope that is in you.

1 Peter 3:14–15

HIS BLESSINGS

IT'S IMPORTANT THAT YOU KEEP ASKING GOD TO SHOW YOU WHAT HE WANTS *YOU* TO DO. If you don't ask, you won't know. It's that simple. For example, God may ask you to take a certain job, stop a certain activity, join a certain church, or change the way you've always done something.

Whatever He asks you to do, remember He does this for your greatest blessing. But you must understand that you may not hear Him speaking to you at all if you are not taking the other steps of obedience He expects all of us to take that are found in His Word. "One who turns away his ear from hearing the law, even his prayer is an abomination" (Proverbs 28:9). It's always good to ask Him to lead you on the path He has for you.

> *My heart wants to obey You in all things, Lord. Show me where I am not doing that. If there are steps of obedience I need to take that I don't understand, I pray You would open my eyes to see the truth and help me to take those steps. I don't want to limit Your blessings upon my life because I am not living in obedience to Your ways.*

⤳ GOD'S PROMISE ⤳
For the LORD God is a sun and shield;
the LORD will give grace and glory;
no good thing will He withhold from those who walk uprightly.

Psalm 84:11

In even the most wonderful of jobs or situations, there are still aspects of it that we don't enjoy. But part of being successful in life means doing things we would rather not. This builds character in us. It makes us disciplined. It forms us into the kind of person God can trust. He wants to bless our lives, but He asks us to be willing to do what He requires.

Whenever you find it difficult to do the things you know you need to, ask the Holy Spirit to help you. Be willing to make the sacrifices necessary for the blessings you want. God leaves it up to you to take the first step in doing the right thing. But when you do, the Holy Spirit will assist you the rest of the way.

Lord, Your Word says that those of us who love Your law will have great peace and nothing will cause us to stumble. I love Your law because I know it is good and it is there for my benefit.

Enable me to live in obedience to each part of it so that I will not stumble and fall. Help me to obey You so that I can dwell in the confidence and peace of knowing I am living Your way. Help me to be ever learning about Your ways so I can live in the fullness of Your presence and move into all the blessings You have for me.

∞ GOD'S PROMISE ∞

Whatever we ask we receive from Him, because we keep His commandments and do those things that are pleasing in His sight.

1 John 3:22

HIS COMFORT

Our spiritual and emotional lives are much the same. When the dark clouds of trial, struggle, grief, or suffering roll in and settle on us so thick that we can barely see ahead of us, it's easy to forget there is a place of calm, light, clarity, and peace we can rise to. If we take God's hand in those difficult times, He will lift us up above our circumstances to the place of comfort, warmth, and safety He has for us.

One of my favorite names for the Holy Spirit is the Comforter. Just as we don't have to beg the sun for light, we don't have to beg the Holy Spirit for comfort either. He *is* comfort. We simply have to separate ourselves from anything that separates us from Him. We have to pray that when we go through difficult times, He will give us a greater sense of His comfort in it.

Lord, help me to remember that no matter how dark or uncertain my situation may become, You are the light of my life and can never be put out. No matter what dark clouds settle on my life, You will lift me above the storm and into the comfort of Your presence.

In times of trial, I pray for an added sense of Your presence. Thank You that I walk before You with hope in my heart and life in my body. You are my Comforter.

❧ GOD'S PROMISE ❧
Wait on the LORD; be of good courage,
and He shall strengthen your heart;
wait, I say, on the LORD.

Psalm 27:14

WHEN WE'RE IN THE MIDST OF TROUBLE, tragedy, loss, devastation, or disappointment, we hurt terribly and find it impossible to think beyond the pain. But the Holy Spirit is there to help us. In other translations of the Bible, He is called the Helper. Jesus said, "I will pray to the Father, and He will give you another Helper, that He may abide with you forever—the Spirit of truth" (John 14:16–17).

When we turn to the Holy Spirit for help and comfort, He will not only give us aid, but He will give us a richer portion of His presence than we have ever had before. We will be blessed even when we mourn, because it will be the Comforter who comforts us.

Lord, help me to remember to give thanks to You in all things, knowing that You reign in the midst of them. Remind me that You have redeemed me and I am Yours and nothing is more important than that. I know when I pass through the waters You will be with me and the river will not overflow me. That's because You are a good God and have sent Your Holy Spirit to comfort and help me.

I pray that You, O God of hope, will fill me with all joy and peace and faith so that I will "abound in hope by the power of the Holy Spirit" (Romans 15:13). Thank You that You have sent Your Holy Spirit to be my Comforter and Helper. Remind me of that in the midst of difficult times.

≈ GOD'S PROMISE ≈

Blessed are the poor in spirit, for theirs is the kingdom of heaven.
Blessed are those who mourn, for they shall be comforted.

Matthew 5:3–4

TEN GOOD REASONS TO READ GOD'S WORD

1. *To know where you are going.* You can't foresee the future or exactly where you are heading, but God's Word will guide you (Psalm 119:133).

2. *To have wisdom.* Knowledge of God's Word is where wisdom begins to grow in you (Psalm 19:7).

3. *To find success.* When you live according to the teachings of the Bible, life works (Joshua 1:8).

4. *To live in purity.* You must live a life of holiness and purity in order to enjoy more of the Lord's presence, but you can't be made pure without being cleansed through God's Word (Psalm 119:9).

5. *To obey God.* If you don't understand what God's laws are, how can you obey them? (Psalm 119:33–35)

6. *To have joy.* You cannot be free of anxiety and unrest without the Word of God in your heart (Psalm 19:8).

7. *To grow in faith.* You can't grow in faith without reading and hearing the Word of God (Romans 10:17).

8. *To find deliverance.* You won't know what you need to be free of unless you study God's Word to find out (John 8:31–32).

9. *To have peace.* God will give you a peace that the world can't give, but you must find it first in His Word (Psalm 119:165).

10. *To distinguish good from evil.* Everything has become so relative today, how can you know for sure what is right and wrong without God's Word? (Psalm 119:11)

RECEIVING DIVINE INSPIRATION

*I*t is no wonder that we aren't able to change ourselves. We don't even understand what we're supposed to be changed to or why. Only God can open our eyes to see these things. That's why we have to pray the "Change me, Lord" prayer. I know it's one of the most frightening and difficult prayers to pray. We'd so much rather pray, "Change him, Lord" or "Change her, Lord." Plus if we give the Lord carte blanche to do whatever He wants in us, God only knows what He might do.

But there is a way we can pray that will change us, and it's not frightening. That is to pray, "Make me more like Christ." Who doesn't want to exhibit the character of Jesus? Who doesn't want to be more like Him in every way?

Lord, I want to be changed, and I pray those changes will begin today. I know I can't change myself in any way that is significant or lasting, but by the transforming power of Your Holy Spirit all things are possible. Grant me, according to the riches of Your glory, to be strengthened with might through Your Spirit in my inner being.

Transform me into Your likeness. I know that You will supply all that I need according to Your riches in Christ.

∾ GOD'S PROMISE ∾

I have been crucified with Christ; it is no longer I who live,
but Christ lives in me; and the life
which I now live in the flesh I live by faith
in the Son of God, who loved me and gave Himself for me.

Galatians 2:20

GOD WANTS TO DO GREAT THINGS THROUGH US if we would just step out in faith when He asks us to. That's why He lets us go through some difficult times. Times when we feel weak and vulnerable. He allows certain things to happen so that we will turn to Him. It's in those times, when we are forced to pray in greater faith, that our faith and our lives are transformed.

When you take the promises and truths in God's Word and declare them out loud, you'll sense your faith increasing. Every time we reach out and touch Him in prayer, our lives are healed, changed, transformed in some way.

> *Lord, soften my heart where it has become hard. Make me fresh where I have become stale. Lead me and instruct me where I have become unteachable, and make me to be faithful and obedient like Jesus was. Where I am resistant to change, help me to trust Your work in my life. Transform me by the power of Your Spirit.*

> *Give me faith so that I can pray in power. I don't want to see a need and then not have faith strong enough to pray and believe for the situation or myself to change.*

∽ GOD'S PROMISE ∽

In this you greatly rejoice, though now for a little while, if need be, you have been grieved by various trials, that the genuineness of your faith, being much more precious than gold that perishes, though it is tested by fire, may be found to praise, honor, and glory at the revelation of Jesus Christ.

1 Peter 1:6–7

THROUGH FORGIVENESS

FORGIVENESS IS A CHOICE WE MUST MAKE
EVERY DAY. We choose to forgive whether we feel like it
or not. It's a decision, not a feeling. If we wait for good
feelings, we could end up waiting a lifetime. If you can
think of someone who is hard to forgive, ask God to give
you a heart of forgiveness for them. Pray for them in all the
ways you can think of to pray. It's amazing how God
softens our hearts when we pray for people. Our anger,
resentment, and hurt turn into love.

Sometimes we blame God for things that have happened. Ask
God to show you if any of these things are true about you.
Don't let unforgiveness limit what God wants to do in your life.

*Lord, help me to be a forgiving person. Show me where I
am not. Expose the recesses of my soul so I won't be locked
up by unforgiveness and jeopardize my future. Make me
understand the depth of Your forgiveness toward me so that
I won't hold back forgiveness from others.*

*Help me to forgive myself for the times I have failed. Enable
me to love my enemies as you have commanded in Your
Word. Teach me to bless those who curse me and persecute
me. Make me a person who is quick to forgive, Lord.*

∽ GOD'S PROMISE ∽
Judge not, and you shall not be judged. Condemn not, and
you shall not be condemned. Forgive, and you will be forgiven.

Luke 6:37

Everything we do in life that has eternal value hinges on two things: loving God and loving others. It's far easier to love God than it is to love others, but God sees them as being the same. One of the most loving things we can do is forgive. It's hard to forgive those who have hurt, offended, or mistreated us. But God wants us to love even our enemies. And in the process of doing so, He perfects us. It's always going to be easy to find things to be unforgiving about. We have to stop looking.

Forgiveness opens your heart and mind and allows the Holy Spirit to work freely in you. It releases you to love God more and feel His love in greater measure. Life is worth nothing without that.

Lord, where there is distance between me and any other family member because of unforgiveness, I pray You would break down that wall. Help me to be an instrument of reconciliation.

Help me to forgive every time I need to do so. I don't want anything to come between You and me, Lord. I choose this day to forgive everyone and everything, and walk free from the death that unforgiveness brings. I know that I cannot be a light to others as long as I am walking in the darkness of unforgiveness. I choose to walk in the light as You are in the light and be cleansed from all sin.

∾ GOD'S PROMISE ∾
If you forgive men their trespasses,
your heavenly Father will also forgive you.
Matthew 6:14

*N*othing we do is more powerful or more life-changing than praising God. It is one of the means by which God transforms us. Every time we praise and worship Him, His presence comes to dwell in us and changes our hearts and allows the Holy Spirit to soften and mold them into whatever He wants them to be.

To experience the joy and power of praise, you must decide to worship the Lord no matter what your circumstances. Of course, the more you get to know God, the easier this becomes. When you get to the point where you can't keep from praising Him, then you are at the place you are supposed to be.

> *Lord, there is no source of greater joy for me than worshiping You. I come into Your presence with thanksgiving and bow before You this day. I exalt Your name for You are great and worthy to be praised.*
>
> *Thank You that "You have put gladness in my heart" (Psalm 4:7). All honor and majesty, strength and glory, holiness and righteousness are Yours, O Lord.*

❧ GOD'S PROMISE ❧

Whoever offers praise glorifies Me; and to him who
orders his conduct aright I will show the salvation of God.

Psalm 50:23

PRAISING AND WORSHIPING GOD WITH OTHER BELIEVERS is one of the most powerful and significant things we can do in our lives. Corporate worship causes bondages to be broken, and it makes the way for wonderful changes in us that might never happen otherwise. A powerful dynamic occurs in the spirit realm when we worship God together that can't happen any other way.

No matter what your church background is or has been, ask God to make you into the true worshiper He wants you to be. Give your whole self to it. The songs of worship you sing over and over in your heart in the day will fill your soul in the night.

Lord, thank You that Your plans for my life are good, and You have a future for me that is full of hope. Thank You that You are always restoring my life to greater wholeness. I praise You and thank You that You are my Healer, my Deliverer, my Provider, my Redeemer, my Father, and my Comforter.

Thank You for revealing Yourself to me through Your Word, through Your Son, Jesus, and through Your mighty works upon the earth and in my life.

~ GOD'S PROMISE ~
Offer to God thanksgiving,
and pay your vows to the Most High.
Call upon Me in the day of trouble;
I will deliver you, and you shall glorify Me.

Psalm 50:14–15

THROUGH DREAMS

GOD WANTS US TO DREAM. He puts dreams in our hearts for His purposes. But in our dreaming, He doesn't want us to exclude Him. God's Word says we will perish if we don't have a vision, but the vision we have must be His. If we don't have a vision from Him, then we don't have a vision that will ever be realized.

God wants us to surrender our dreams because we can't be led by Him if we are chasing after a dream of our own making. And He wants us to surrender all of them. That way He can tell us which of them are in line with His will. If they are only our dreams and visions and not His, we will experience a lifetime of unfulfillment trying to make them happen. When the dream in our heart is the one He put there, we will be inspired to pursue it His way.

> *Lord, I release all my hopes and dreams to You this day. If there is anything that I am longing for that is not to be a part of my life, I ask You to take away the desire for it so that what should be in my life will be released to me. I realize how dangerous it is to make idols of my dreams— to try and force my life to be what I have envisioned for myself. I lift up to you all that I desire, and I declare this day that what I desire most is Your will in my life.*
>
> *I look forward to watching the dreams You have for my life unfold as I follow in Your ways and receive divine inspiration from You.*

❧ GOD'S PROMISE ❧

Beloved, now we are children of God; and it has not yet been revealed what we shall be, but we know that when He is revealed, we shall be like Him, for we shall see Him as He is.

1 John 3:2

*W*hen God wants to make changes in our lives, and we're willing to let Him, He starts by cutting away all that is unnecessary. In this process, He strips from us everything that could hinder our future growth in order to prepare us to bring forth good fruit. Our life may look barren during that time, but God is actually freeing us from anything that does not bring forth life.

We don't want to be wishful thinkers, always living in a dream-world and never seeing anything of significance materialize. We want to live with confidence that our hopes, dreams, and expectations are based on God-given certainty that He is behind them. We want the hope that comes from God alone, a hope that is built on a foundation of His promises to us and His revealed purposes in us. This kind of hope is an anchor to the soul.

Lord, I want the desires of my heart to line up with the desires of Your heart. As hard as it is for me to let go of the hopes and dreams I have for my life, I lay them all at Your feet. I accept Your decision and fully submit to it. Lead me in Your path, Lord. I don't want to speak a vision of my own heart (Jeremiah 23:16). Give me a vision for the future and plant hope in my heart.

Whenever I face times of change and transition, I will seek Your guidance. I long to walk with You and see the wonders up ahead that You have in store for me. Even as I face trials, I know that You protect me and love me. Thank You for caring about every detail of my life and fulfilling Your plans for me.

∾ GOD'S PROMISE ∾
Where there is no vision, the people perish.

Proverbs 29:18 KJV

*J*I have come to know that God can smooth my path, calm the storms, keep me and all I care about safe, and even make my way simple when I ask Him to carry the complexities of life for me. But these things don't just happen. Not without prayer.

Prayer helps us live God's way and not our own. It lifts our eyes from the temporal to the eternal and shows us what is really important. It will give us the ability to distinguish the truth from a lie. It will strengthen our faith and encourage us to believe for the impossible. It will inspire and enable us to become the obedient child of God we long to be and believe we can be.

Lord, You have said in Your Word that whoever believes in You will have rivers of living water flowing from their heart (John 7:38). I believe in You, and I long for Your living water to flow in and through me today and every day that I'm alive.

I invite Your Holy Spirit to fill me afresh right now. Just as a spring is constantly being renewed with fresh water so that it stays pure, I ask You to renew me in that same way today. I invite, You, Holy Spirit, to pray through me. Help me in my weakness. Teach me the things I don't know about You.

∽ GOD'S PROMISE ∽
We have this treasure in earthen vessels, that the
excellence of the power may be of God and not of us.

2 Corinthians 4:7

DO YOU HUNGER FOR A GREATER SENSE OF THE LORD'S PRESENCE IN YOUR LIFE? Do you desire to know God in a deeper way? The good news is that God wants you to long for His presence. He wants you to find your fulfillment in Him. He wants you to walk closely with Him. He wants you to put all your hopes and dreams in His hands and look to Him to meet all of your needs. When you do, He will open the storehouse of blessing upon your life. That's because these things are His will for you.

And these things will happen, but only when you commit to prayer.

Lord, I look to You for everything I need in my life. Help me to put all my expectations in You. I am desperately aware of how much I need Your power to transform me and my circumstances. You sent Your Holy Spirit so that I could live in power. Help me to fulfill that promise. You gave Your life for me because You loved me. Help me to do the same.

I long for Your presence, Lord. Help me turn my eyes, my thoughts, and my sincere prayers to You.

∽ GOD'S PROMISE ∽
Until now you have asked nothing in My name.
Ask, and you will receive, that your joy may be full.

John 16:24

TWENTY GOOD REASONS TO WORSHIP GOD

1. *He forgives my iniquities.*

2. *He heals all my diseases.*

3. *He redeems my life from destruction.*

4. *He crowns me with lovingkindness.*

5. *He satisfies my mouth with good things.*

6. *He executes righteousness and justice for the oppressed.*

7. *He makes His ways known.*

8. *He is merciful.*

9. *He is gracious.*

10. *He is slow to anger.*

11. *He will not strive with us.*

12. *He will not keep His anger forever.*

13. *He does not punish us according to our iniquities.*

14. *He shows great mercy to those who fear Him.*

15. *He removes our transgressions from us.*

16. *He has pity on us.*

17. *He remembers we are dust.*

18. *His mercy is everlasting.*

19. *He blesses our children and grandchildren who obey Him.*

20. *He rules over all and His throne is established.*

LIVING THE GOOD LIFE

*I*t doesn't matter if your work is recognized by the whole world, or if only God sees it. It doesn't matter if you are getting paid big bucks, or you are receiving no financial compensation whatsoever. Your work is valuable. And you want it to be blessed by God. That's why it is good to pray about it often.

Prayer helps us to find the balance between being "greedy for gain," which depletes our life (Proverbs 1:19), and having "a slack hand," which makes us poor (Proverbs 10:4). Prayer helps us to not "overwork to be rich" (Proverbs 23:4–5) yet still be diligent in our work, which may ultimately bring us monetary rewards (Proverbs 10:4). Prayer helps us find the balance between laziness and obsession, between gaining the whole world and losing our own soul (Matthew 16:26).

Lord, as I look to my future, I hope to serve You and others with the work I do. I pray You would always show me what work I am supposed to be doing, and give me the strength and energy to get it done well. Develop in me the skills I need, and enable me to do what I do successfully.

May my steps toward the future be taken with Your guidance. May I find great fulfillment and satisfaction in every aspect of the work You have planned for me to do.

⤳ GOD'S PROMISE ⤳
The labor of the righteous leads to life.

Proverbs 10:16

YOUR WORK IS IMPORTANT TO GOD, it's important to others, and it's important to you. You can't afford not to pray about it. Commit your work to the Lord and ask Him to bless it. But remember that sometimes the reward for your work is in the actual doing of it itself. You don't get paid for maintaining a home, serving at the rescue mission, or teaching a child to read, but the reward for seeing the result of your labor is priceless.

Ask God what He wants you to do. And in everything you do, give God the glory. Pray that God will help you do your job well and make your work fruitful, successful, and fulfilling.

Lord, I commit my work to You, knowing You will establish it. May it always be that I love the work I do and be able to do the work I love. According to Your Word I pray that I will not lag in diligence in my work, but remain fervent in spirit, serving You in everything I do.

Establish the work of my hands so that what I do will find favor with others and be a blessing for many. May it always be glorifying to You.

❧ GOD'S PROMISE ❧

Blessed is every one who fears the LORD, who walks in His ways.
When you eat the labor of your hands, you shall be happy,
and it shall be well with you.

Psalm 128:1–2

GOOD RELATIONSHIPS

GOD CREATED US TO BE IN FAMILIES. We have a natural hunger to be a part of something that gives us a sense of acceptance, affirmation, and being needed and appreciated. But even if we have never received that from our own biological families, there is good news. God sets us in spiritual families, and in many ways this can be just as important.

God is our Father. We are God's kids. That means we who are believers in Jesus are all brothers and sisters. There are too many of us to all live in the same house, so God puts us in separate houses—they are called churches. Our relationships within these church families are crucial to our well-being. We can never reach our full destiny apart from the people God puts in our lives.

Lord, I lift up every one of my relationships to You and ask You to bless them. I pray that each one would be glorifying to You. Help me to choose my friends wisely so I won't be led astray. Give me discernment and strength to separate myself from anyone who is not a good influence.

I release all my relationships to You and pray that Your will be done in each of them. Bless those who are a part of both my biological and spiritual families.

☙ GOD'S PROMISE ❧
You are no longer strangers and foreigners, but fellow citizens with the saints and members of the household of God, having been built on the foundation of the apostles and prophets, Jesus Christ Himself being the chief cornerstone.

Ephesians 2:19–20

It's important to be yoked with people who walk closely with God. Accountability results from having close relationships with strong believers who are themselves accountable to other strong believers. It's important to be accountable because we are all capable of being deceived. We all have blind spots. We need people who will help us see the truth about ourselves and our lives. And we need to have the kind of relationships that don't break down when truth is spoken in love.

This doesn't mean that we should have nothing to do with non-believers. Far from it. We are God's tool to reach others for His kingdom. But our closest relationships, the ones that influence us the most, need to be with people who love and fear God. If you do not have these, pray for godly friends to come into your life. And be sure to *be* a godly friend to those you encounter.

Lord, I pray for godly friends, role models, and mentors to come into my life. Send people who will speak the truth in love. I pray especially that there will be women in my life who are trustworthy, kind, loving, and faithful. Most of all I pray that they be women of strong faith who will add to my life and I to theirs. May we mutually raise the standards to which we aspire.

May forgiveness and love flow freely between us. Make me to be Your light in all my relationships.

❧ GOD'S PROMISE ❧
God sets the solitary in families;
He brings out those who are bound into prosperity.

Psalm 68:6

Women want to live fruitful lives. They want to be unshakable in God's truth yet moved by the suffering and needs of others. They want to know God in all the ways He can be known, and they want to be transformed by the power of His Spirit. But they are often hard on themselves when they don't see all these things happening on a daily basis. They often observe all they are doing wrong and don't notice all they are doing right.

For that reason, we have to pray about our attitude. We must ask God to help us be happily expectant, unwaveringly hopeful, and always uplifted. And we must be that way for ourselves as well as others. God is preparing you for the important work He has ahead for you to do. Ask Him to make your attitude right so you can be ready.

Lord, I come humbly before You and ask You to cleanse my mind of all wrong thinking and renew a right spirit within me. Forgive me for thoughts I have had, words I have spoken, and things that I have done that are not glorifying to You, or are in direct contradiction to Your commands. I want to be changed so that I can be prepared for all that you have in store for me.

I know that You are "gracious and merciful, slow to anger and of great kindness" (Joel 2:13). Forgive me for ever taking that for granted. Your mercy has changed my life.

❧ GOD'S PROMISE ❧

If we confess our sins, He is faithful and just to forgive us our sins
and to cleanse us from all unrighteousness.

1 John 1:9

NOTHING IS HEAVIER THAN SIN. We don't realize how heavy it is until the day we feel its crushing weight bringing death to our souls. We don't see how destructive it is until we smash into the wall that has gone up between us and God because of it. That's why it's best to confess every sin as soon as we are aware of it and get our hearts cleansed and right immediately.

Confession gets sin out in the open before God. When you confess your sin, you're not informing God of something He doesn't know. He already knows. He wants to know that you know. Confessing, however, is more than just apologizing. Anyone can do that. But true confession means admitting in full detail what you have done and then fully *repenting* of it.

Lord, show me any place in my life where I harbor sin in my thoughts, words, or actions that I have not recognized. Show me the truth about myself so that I can see it clearly. Examine my soul and expose my motives to reveal what I need to understand.

Enable me to make changes where I need to do so. Open my eyes to what I need to see so that I can confess all sin and repent of it. I want to cleanse my hands and purify my heart as You have commanded in Your Word.

⤜ GOD'S PROMISE ⤛
Come near to God and he will come near to you.
Wash your hands, you sinners, and purify your hearts,
you double-minded.

James 4:8 NIV

GOOD PROTECTION

PERSONALLY, I BELIEVE OUR HEAVENLY FATHER LOOKS OUT FOR US and protects us from danger far more than we realize. But it's not something we can take for granted. It's something we must pray about often.

Part of being protected by God has to do with obeying Him and living in His will. When we don't do either of those things, we come out from under the umbrella of His covering. We don't hear His voice telling us which way to go. How many times might people have been spared from something disastrous if they had only asked God to show them what to do and then obeyed Him.

Lord, I pray for Your hand of protection to be upon me. I trust in Your Word, which assures me that You are my rock, my fortress, my deliverer, my shield, my stronghold, and my strength in whom I trust.

Help me to never stray from the center of Your will or off the path You have for me. Enable me to always hear Your voice guiding me. You, Lord, are my refuge and strength and "a very present help in trouble." Your peace calms my fears and offers me assurance in every circumstance.

❧ GOD'S PROMISE ❧

Because you have made the LORD, who is my refuge,
even the Most high, your habitation, no evil shall befall you,
nor shall any plague come near your dwelling.

Psalm 91:9–10

In those precarious moments, when your future is hanging in the balance, you want the confidence of knowing you have been communicating with your heavenly Father all along and He has His eye on you. These are the times when you need a prayer answered instantly. But in order for that to happen, you must be praying ongoingly.

God is a place of safety you can run to, but it helps if you are running to Him on a daily basis so that you are in familiar territory. The Bible says, "In the fear of the LORD there is strong confidence, and His children will have a place of refuge. The fear of the LORD is a fountain of life, to avoid the snares of death" (Proverbs 14:26–27). When we have our eyes on God, He keeps an eye on us.

> *"Be merciful to me, O God, be merciful to me! For my soul trusts in You; and in the shadow of Your wings I will make my refuge" (Psalm 57:1). Thank You that "I will both lie down in peace, and sleep; for You alone, O LORD, make me dwell in safety" (Psalm 4:8). Thank You for Your promises of protection. I lay claim to them this day and for the rest of my life.*
>
> *I praise You, Lord. You mightily defend me and Your heart is my refuge. Thank You for being an ever-present source of comfort and strength. I rest my life in Your hands.*

❧ GOD'S PROMISE ❧
He shall give His angels charge over you,
to keep you in all your ways.

Psalm 91:11

All of us are planting something in our lives every single day, whether we realize it or not. And we are also reaping whatever we have planted in the past. The quality of our lives right now is the result of what we planted and harvested some time before. We reap the good and the bad for years after we have sown. That's why it is so important to plant and nurture the right seeds now.

Jesus said that He is the vine and you and I are the branches. If we abide in Him we will bear fruit. "Abide" means to remain, to stay, to dwell. In other words, if we dwell with Him and He dwells with us, we will bear the fruit of His Spirit. And that is the greatest harvest we could hope for.

Lord, plant the fruit of Your Spirit in me and cause it to flourish. Help me to abide in You, Jesus, so that I will bear fruit in my life. I invite You, Holy Spirit, to fill me afresh with Your love today so that it will flow out of me and into the lives of others.

Knowing You brings me joy. Make me patient with others so that I reflect this joy and Your character to them. Help me to be kind whenever there is opportunity for it, and may Your goodness flow through me so that I will do good to everyone.

∾ GOD'S PROMISE ∾

The fruit of the Spirit is love, joy, peace, longsuffering, kindness, goodness, faithfulness, gentleness, self-control.

Galatians 5:22

IF YOU'VE NOT BEEN BEARING THE FRUIT OF THE SPIRIT IN YOUR LIFE THE WAY YOU'D LIKE, ask God to help you plant good seeds and pull up any weeds that may have grown up around your soul. Feed the soil of your heart with the food of God's Word and ask the Holy Spirit to water it afresh every day. As long as you abide faithfully in the true Vine, I guarantee you'll produce a crop of spiritual fruit that will make your heavenly Father proud.

Lord, where I need to be pruned in order to bear more fruit, I submit myself to You. I know that without You I can do nothing. You are the Vine and I am the branch. I must abide in You in order to bear fruit. Help me to do that. Thank You for Your promise that if I abide in You and Your Word abides in me, I can ask what I desire and it will be done for me (John 15:7).

May I be like a tree planted by the rivers of Your living water so I will bring forth fruit in season that won't wither (Psalm 1:3). In Jesus' name, I ask that the fruit of Your Spirit will grow in me and be recognized clearly by all who see me so that it glorifies You.

❧ GOD'S PROMISE ❧

I am the true vine, and My Father is the vinedresser.
Every branch in Me that does not bear fruit He takes away; and every branch that bears fruit He prunes, that it may bear more fruit.
You are already clean because of the word which I have spoken to you.
Abide in Me, and I in you. As the branch cannot bear fruit of itself, unless it abides in the vine, neither can you, unless you abide in Me.

John 15:1–4

EIGHT GOOD THINGS TO THINK ABOUT DAILY

(From Philippians 4:8)

1. *Whatever things are true.* If you think about what is honest, genuine, authentic, sincere, faithful, accurate, and truthful, then you won't be saying anything false, incorrect, erroneous, deceitful, or untrue.

2. *Whatever things are noble.* If you think about what is admirable, high quality, excellent, magnanimous, superior, or honorable, then you won't be saying anything that is base, petty, mean, dishonorable, or low-minded.

3. *Whatever things are just.* If you think about what is fair, reasonable, equitable, proper, lawful, right, correct, deserved, upright, honorable, and seemly, then you won't be saying anything that is unjustified, biased, unreasonable, unlawful, or unfair.

4. *Whatever things are pure.* If you think about what is clean, clear, spotless, chaste, unsullied, undefiled, or untainted with evil, then you won't be saying anything that is inferior, tainted, adulterated, defiled, polluted, corrupted, tarnished, or unholy.

5. *Whatever things are lovely.* If you think about what is pleasing, agreeable, charming, satisfying, or splendid, then you won't be saying anything that is unpleasant, offensive, disagreeable, revolting, unlovely, ominous, or ugly.

6. *Whatever things are of good report.* If you think about what is admirable, winsome, worthwhile, recommended, positive, or worthy of repeating, then you won't be saying anything that is negative, discouraging, undesirable, or full of bad news, gossip, and rumor.

7. *Whatever things are virtuous.* If you think about what is moral, ethical, upright, excellent, good, impressive, or conforming to high moral standards, then you won't be saying anything that is depraved, unethical, licentious, bad, self-indulgent, dissipated, evil, or immoral.

8. *Whatever things are praiseworthy.* If you think about what is laudable, admirable, commendable, valuable, acclaimed, applauded, glorified, exalted, honored, or approved of, then you won't be saying anything that is critical, condemning, deprecating, disapproving, disparaging, denouncing, belittling, or depressing.